AFRICAN DOCTOR

AFRICAN DOCTOR

By

DR. T. GERALD GARRY, M.B.E.

THE BOOK CLUB

121 CHARING CROSS ROAD LONDON W.C.2.

First published 1939

MADE AND PRINTED IN GREAT BRITAIN BY
EBENEZER BAYLIS AND SON, LTD., THE
TRINITY PRESS, WORCESTER, AND LONDON

TO
BLANCHE

I

I BECAME a medical student in the early eighties, when a doctor's training was very different from what it is to-day. At Queen's College, Galway, where I began my studies, the curriculum for the first year comprised Botany, Zoology, French and Physics. It seems rather a strange beginning to a medical career now. The Professors varied extremely in ability and popularity. Both French and German were taught by a German Professor who was much disliked by most of the students. At that time the Prussians were not much loved in Ireland, and I doubt whether the national feeling has changed since then. One day this man asked a student to read aloud a passage from a French book. When he had finished, he made some insulting remarks about the hopelessness of teaching French to the Irish. All the students rose as one man and left the lecture room, singing, at my instigation, the "Marseillaise". That evening we attacked his private residence, broke all the windows and did it considerable damage. We would have done more but for the interference of the police. He took his revenge later, however, by ploughing us unmercifully in the examinations.

But for the sake of the reputation of that illustrious seat of learning, I hasten to add that many of the other professors were men of quite a different type. "Old Melville", the Professor of Chemistry, was in many respects a strange character, but with all his peculiarities he was a lovable old fellow and extremely popular with the students. Perhaps this came to some extent from his reputation of never having ploughed a student in an examination, certainly one of his most popular characteristics. He also had the reputation of never having been seen to smile. The nearest approach to one ever seen on his face was when I asked him the chemical composition of potheen, and which he considered worse for the nervous system, potheen or Scotch whisky (the latter being his favourite beverage). Once on his birthday we made a more determined effort to get the gloomy professor to relax, as the Americans would say. We serenaded him and presented him with a bottle of potheen and a beautiful bouquet of flowers with the thistle and the shamrock most artistically arranged, the former being a graceful reference to his Scotch ancestry. The deputation was headed by a blind piper playing "Ye banks and braes of bonnee Dundee". This time the dour Scotch professor really did relax and thoroughly enjoyed the compliment and the joke. He certainly deserved it. There are not many professors who can boast of having the reputation of never having ploughed a student.

Owing something perhaps to his kind attention, I left Galway to continue my studies in Dublin.

There the teaching and the life of the students were quite different from that in the smaller centre, although the change was not in every respect for the better. In Galway, opportunities for practice in hospital were very limited but it had considerable advantages as regards purely theoretical work. The professors as a rule were only too willing to assist and encourage the student, conditions which did not always exist in the medical schools in Dublin. They were then very numerous, far too numerous for their efficiency and financial stability. At that time the professors in all the Dublin schools delivered the prescribed lectures and then disappeared as soon as they could to attend to their hospital or private practice. Whole time professors were a rarity. The upshot was that students were left to their own devices or else to place themselves under the guidance of a "grind" or coach, a most pernicious form of cramming. It deprives the student of all initiative and reasoning power as well as self-confidence, the most essential trait in the character of a medical practitioner. But what is the average student to do if deprived of the assistance of professors? He must do as I did—attend a "grind's" séance out of curiosity and then fall back on the very best text books, and if you are in doubt about anything, consult the professor (if an examiner, he will not forget your zeal and that goes a long way sometimes).

By the system of cramming, the mind is filled with the fallacies as well as the facts required for examinations. It is developed so thoroughly in some places that the foibles of examiners are studied and catalogued. Then the unfortunate student is given precise and detailed instructions concerning the respective items which he must be "well up in" when confronted by Professors X., Y. or Z. He is also told not to be too prompt in answering questions, as the examiners only have a limited amount of time at their disposal for each candidate in a *viva voce* examination. What has all this to do with the training of an efficient doctor?

The Dublin School of Medicine deservedly enjoyed a great reputation for more than two centuries. At one time it was threatened by the establishment of many small teaching centres, or "schools" as they were also called. Fortunately some of these have died a natural death but there is room for further scrapping. Now that money is flowing to Dublin because of the Hospital Sweepstake, many of the small antiquated hospitals ought to be eliminated and one large central institution created fitted with all the latest modern improvements in the way of apparatus and equipment.

In the last century, the reputation of the Dublin School was largely due to such eminent physicians as William Stokes, Robert James Graves and Dominie Carrigan.

Stokes was a very remarkable man, according to Carlyle "a rather fierce, sinister looking man, very emphatic and contradictory". But Carlyle's opinion carried little weight with Stokes's fellow countrymen, who well knew that no needy patient ever sought his assistance in vain and that no heart was too heavy for him to attempt to lighten its burden. While still a student in 1825, he published a treatise entitled *Introduction to the use of the Stethoscope* which brought him £70 but also much ridicule from his teacher, Alison, for wasting his time on such a worthless instrument. In 1826 he worked with Graves who gave his name to the now well known disease. These two eminent doctors fought together the typhus epidemic in Dublin in that year, as well as the Asiatic cholera scourge that swept Ireland in 1832.

These two doctors are of especial interest to me as I knew later so many of their descendants, from Colonel A. Stokes of the Egyptian Army to Robert Graves, the well known author of *Good-bye to all that*. The latter was at one time Professor of Literature at Cairo University and on many occasions I noticed his pugnacious idealism at odds with the conservatism of his less imaginative colleagues.

But to return to the Dublin School or Schools of Medicine. As I have already said, many of the smaller hospitals should be scrapped in the interests of economy and efficiency. The matter is far too serious for sentiment and personal interests and prejudices to be considered. In the past, conditions were different in every respect. These small hospitals played a useful part in the training of efficient doctors. In my time, a student could join a particular hospital and yet be quite free, even welcome, to go the rounds and attend operations or clinical lectures at any of the others. I doubt whether such fraternal feelings between a group of hospitals existed anywhere else, and it certainly does not exist to-day. I took full advantage of this arrangement. In this way I imbibed the teaching of such well known physicians as Sir Christopher Nixon, the precise and dogmatic Jimmy Little, the sarcastic Foote and the ever amiable Sammy Gordon.

My regular professor of Medicine was R. D. Lyons, a Liberal M.P. He was an army doctor and had served in the Crimea War. He was a fluent speaker but almost invariably discussed "Fevers", especially Spotted Fever, Typhus or Dysentery (not the Dysenteries as not much was known about them until the Great War). He would have been surprised if I had told him in an examination what I now know to be the truth, that lice killed more British and French soldiers in the Crimea than the Russians. This was certainly the case, and furthermore the louse has probably won far more wars in the past than military generals.

The various hospitals worked extraordinarily well together at that time, although keen rivalry must have existed between them to attract students, for it meant more money for them in the way of fees. But I cannot remember the staff of one hospital making unkind criticisms of another at that time. A true gentlemen's agreement seemed to exist between them, long before the politicians thought of making—and breaking—such a thing. Later in my career I found that such high ethical standards do not always exist in the profession, and in fact are more uncommon than one likes to acknowledge. The worst case I ever came across was when I once consulted a very famous titled surgeon, now dead, about a most serious case. He gave me his opinion but could not undertake the required treatment himself. So far, so good; but then he tried to persuade me to put the case in the hands of a surgeon who was a friend of his, a man in whom I had no confidence. I refused and called in another surgeon myself. This distinguished medical Knight then met the patient's husband and invited him to meet his friend, with whom he was staying, suggesting that he was the man who should operate on his wife. As a result of this meeting, I was asked to put the case in his hands. I refused to do so and said that I would resign from the case, which I did. The husband then came to see me and implored me to accept this surgeon out of consideration for his personal feelings which were obviously profound and sincere. I reluctantly gave in. The patient finally recovered, in spite of the turmoil caused by the non-observance of the fundamental rules of medical etiquette by the leader of a great teaching centre.

The life of a medical student in Dublin in the eighties

of the last century was very different from that of to-day. It was more hilarious, probably more picturesque and certainly more squalid. Only a very small percentage of the students ever qualified, perhaps not more than twenty per cent. What became of the rest was a complete mystery to me. When an early death did not offer a simple solution to the problem of a livelihood, they just disappeared without leaving a trace behind them. Shortly after qualifying, I was in Boston U.S.A. when three shabbily dressed individuals called on me on board the boat. Their complexions revealed their mode of living and their errand of course was to borrow money. I remembered them as three of the most brilliant students of my first year, who had actually passed "the half" before taking the wrong track. How they found me out, I could never understand but the ingenuity of such men when there is a drink in prospect is amazing.

There were always innumerable "chronics" leading a hopelessly precarious existence. At the beginning of each session, they lay in wait for new students who were generally unsophisticated and had plenty of money. Like all addicts whether of drink or drugs, they took immense delight in dragging others down to their own level. Lending money of course hastened the ruin of the fresh students. If properly conducted hostels had been attached to the hospitals, many dismal tragedies would have been averted. As it was, students were forced to live in cheerless digs on badly cooked food, not always cleanly served. There was no supervision of any kind and it was thus not surprising that many young students made the worst possible use of their time.

Besides the two classes of students, the workers and

the derelicts, there was another class of considerable interest from the psychological point of view. These men usually led a riotous life for the greater part of the session and then suddenly disappeared from the social orbit. They had gone to earth to work hard for the coming examination which they frequently passed with distinction. Many of them subsequently did extremely well in their professions. I remember one man of this kind who became a famous judge. Perhaps his skill in making a speech on any subject under the sun while standing on a table after his second drink, had been a good training for him to deliver judgments from the bench.

Not all of these energetic students, however, got qualified in their native country. Many of them went to Edinburgh for reasons best known to themselves. At that time the Scotch diploma was not considered of much account. But it granted the recipient full legal rights to experiment with the health and lives of the community, and in the opinion of some students, what else mattered? The periodic departure of students from Dublin to Edinburgh was always observed as a great event. Crowds of us would go to the North Wall to give them a cheerful send off, and also to offer them a parting drink which we knew perfectly well they would refuse, as they were in strict training for the forthcoming entrance tests. But they had no objection to borrowing a quid which they promised to repay out of their first fees, for they were all perfectly certain to pass and I cannot recall a single failure.

The exodus often had an amusing sequel. After some weeks our old friends would appear in the streets, usually in tall hats and frock coats, now fully fledged "doctors". They generally passed us without a sign of recognition. When they did condescend to speak, their manner was most patronizing and they were even said to speak sometimes with a strong Scotch accent. The rapid metamorphosis from wild young student to sedate, black coated and even pompous doctor was often amazing. It was difficult not to laugh at the urbane manner, calm dignity and Scotch accent of a man who only a few weeks before had been the witty and rollicking toastmaster of the famous pub, "The Hole in the Wall". But in my opinion, it is the wildest and most adventurous students who often turn out the best, most humane and generous doctors. I have little taste for the man who boasts that he never entered a pub in his life or took part in the riotous assemblies inseparable from student life at all times in all countries. He is not the sort of man who makes a good doctor with wide human sympathies and becomes the friend and confident of his fellow men.

But besides the general life of the students, the very system of medical education was naturally completely different from what it is now. Whether the present system is a better one is quite another matter. Personally, I very much doubt it. Whatever advances there may have been in the practice of medicine and surgery since then, they do not necessarily mean that the fundamental principles of medical education have advanced with them. In some respects, I do not hesitate to say that they have deteriorated. For the final examination at the Royal University, the subjects included Advanced Anatomy, Physiology, Medicine, Surgery, Obstetrics, Gynæcology, Diseases of Children and Medical Jurisprudence. There were written papers as well as practical examinations in all these subjects and failure in any one subject meant rejection in the whole examination. What is the position to-day? The curriculum is certainly more comprehensive but it is encumbered with subjects of very little practical use. Moreover, the student is allowed to take the examination in parts, passing in one or two subjects at a time which is comparatively easily done by the pernicious system of intensive cramming. Then much time is wasted on vaccines in which very few people really believe. To a lesser degree the same thing can be said about serums. The importance of laboratory diagnosis is becoming more and more stressed by examiners and professors. They impress it so much on the unfortunate student that the far greater value of physical signs and symptoms as observed at the bedside are neglected with lamentable results. These physical indications of disease were unquestionably more carefully and thoroughly investigated and more accurately interpreted in the last century than they are to-day. In the vast forests that have so recently been discovered in every sphere of medicine, there are times when the modern doctor seems unable to see the wood for the trees.

For instance, the old clinician emphasized the importance of gaining the confidence of his patient. The present day claptrap of psychical factors was never heard of then, but now it is seriously suggested that we should leave the safe waters chartered by the Fathers of Medicine and cruise in dangerous unknown seas with psycho-analysis for compass, Mrs. Eddy for pilot and vitamen's experts in the crow's-nest, relieved occasionally by an osteopath on the look out for the elusive lesion. Psychology can be a good servant if kept in its proper place as an assistant to cure mental disease, but it is a bad and tyrannical master if allowed to govern the whole kingdom of medicine.

All sense of proportion seems to have been lost. People are encouraged to consult a psychologist now when all they really want is a liver pill. I have no desire to decry the enormous advances made by serious students in their knowledge of the human mind of recent years. It is in the application of their discoveries in ordinary practice that they often seem to me to go astray. I am old-fashioned enough to believe that the well-being of the patient is the first consideration, and this is not always achieved by trying the latest experiments on him.

Although the period of study for a degree has been extended from four years to five, the innumerable subjects now required means that the average student only has an imperfect knowledge of most of them. Then he has acquired it so rapidly, such a multitude of facts have been crammed into him in so short a time that he soon forgets more than half of his superficial knowledge. Whatever may be the exigences of modern medical science, more attention should be paid to the mental digestion of the ordinary student. Like an over-trained athlete, he becomes stale before the event. Or perhaps more accurately I might compare him to a goose which the examiners are stuffing with food in preparation for making him into *paté de foie gras*. However good the *foie gras* may be when they examine it, their treatment has meant acute indigestion for the poor animal when alive, and to obtain what they consider so magnificent a result, he has been killed in the process. Many promising young doctors are killed now by the contemporary examination system, or at least not nearly so well prepared for general work in their profession as they were in the past. For instance, consider the very important subject of Materia Medica, which relates to drugs and their therapeutic value. It was thoroughly taught in my time and at the *viva voce* we had to write prescriptions in dog Latin and English. One serious mistake about dosage or the incompatibility of certain drugs was fatal. But this is not the case to-day. Now the subject is neglected or at all events insufficiently taught, perhaps because the professors have not the same faith in the efficacy of drugs as their predecessors. If proof is needed that doctors are neglecting this subject, you have only to ask the opinion of any dispensing chemist. I have seen prescriptions written by young physicians of wide repute in London that would disgrace a third year student. They were shown to me by dispensing chemists, and it was not at all pleasant to hear their disparaging remarks about the incompetence of the younger generation as prescribers.

You hardly ever see an elegant prescription nowadays. I use the adjective on purpose, for strange as it may seem to some modern practitioners, there is a definite art in writing a good prescription. But now many doctors, and especially foreign doctors, prescribe a proprietary medicine which has been strongly recommended and widely advertised by the manufacturing chemists themselves. If they happen to lose the brochure which they have received with the samples, they are done for. These trade samples with their accompanying advertisements are a serious and growing evil. Any sensible doctor if he had been properly grounded in Materia Medica would put them straight into the waste paper basket, but this seldom seems to be done now. There is an obvious reason. What is a man to do if he cannot write an ordinary prescription himself? The proprietary brands of medicine are a perfect godsend to him. It is not surprising that he makes such wide use of them to cover up his own ignorance.

I am convinced that the great flaw in modern medical education is this lack of any proper training in the use and therapeutic value of drugs. Vegetable drugs are even more discarded than the mineral. And yet, if you consult the ancient systems of medicine, you find that the great nations of antiquity believed that the gods were the first herbalists and had taught the people of the world the art of healing by means of plants and herbs? Is this belief to be regarded now as nothing but a barbaric superstition? Is there not greater truth in it than in many of the new-fangled notions of such shortlived popularity? It is significant that the decline of Egyptian medicine began when mystical formulæ and incantations took the place of the pharmaceutical remedies to be found mentioned in the oldest documents. We see something of the same tendency to-day, more refined and scientific methods (the so-called psychical factors) taking the place of the magic incantations of the past. As a cure for disease, in spite of the blind faith of this scientific age, they amount much to the same thing.

In reading the lives of the great clinicians of the past, nothing is more remarkable than their belief in the efficacy of drugs, based on sound principles and proved to them by practical experiment. Examples could be cited of great reputations being established by the correct administration of some drug now rarely prescribed, and never by some practitioners. Are we now to believe these fine reputations were complete frauds? Was not their work of some value? Is there nothing in it from which we could learn to-day? Their drugs achieved fully authenticated results. They unquestionably cured people of certain diseases. Why consider their painfully acquired knowledge as so much limbo of the past?

Take antimony as an example. Famous physicians have testified to its great value. I can fully corroborate this from personal experience; in fact, I have witnessed many cases of threatened pneumonia averted by its use. I have asked many prescribing chemists whether the younger generation of doctors are in the habit of prescribing this useful drug and the answer is always in the negative.

Practical obstetrics is another subject shamefully neglected to-day; indeed it has been at all times and yet it is the most important branch of the art of medicine. In my time, attendance was only required at ten cases of natural labour; but those who became general practitioners attended Post-graduate Courses to make up for this insufficient training. From what I can see, there has been no improvement in the training for Practical Midwifery; indeed, I think it is worse. For one thing, all this pre-natal fuss about pelvic measurements and such things must have an extremely bad effect on the mental outlook of the pregnant woman who should be taught to look on her confinement as a perfectly natural function.

In face of the facts, something must be wrong somewhere. Hygiene and cleanliness have undoubtedly improved both in Institutions and elsewhere, and yet the death rate from puerperal fever has not appreciably diminished. Without going into details, it is not difficult to realize that much of the chronic invalidism to be found among countless women must be due to unskilful treatment at childbirth, which in its turn must be the result of imperfect training of the doctor. From personal experience, I know this to be a fact. I recently came across an interesting sidelight on this serious matter. It was an advertisement in a medical paper. A fully qualified doctor was advertising for instruction in the use of the forceps.

But one improvement I willingly accord modern medicine, and that is the way in which examinations are now held. In the old days, I cannot deny that some examiners had favourites among the students to whose success they were not quite impartial. Nor will I deny that a certain amount of strategy played an important part in the final issue, but perhaps it still does to-day. For instance, I had been asked to diagnose a case in hospital when the examiner was called away for a moment. I seized the opportunity of asking the patient what was the matter with him according to the doctor. He replied without any hesitation: "Ulster in the stomach". When the doctor returned, I replied likewise, if in slightly different language.

On another occasion, I was asked to perform an extremely difficult operation on the cadaver in the surgical section. It was an operation which the examiner was known to have perfected himself. After choosing the necessary instruments (and incidentally wasting as much time as possible in doing so, as there was a time limit for each student), I blandly turned to him and said: "Sir, this is a very serious operation and if I were ever called upon to perform it, I would decline and call you in immediately". The great man was flattered, if somewhat perplexed for a suitable reply. He finally listened with a contented smile to my description of the various stages of the operation and then asked me to amputate the big toe.

But such tricks would doubtless be more difficult to play now. Extern examiners, that is to say examiners from other hospitals, are employed now and this eliminates any chance of favouritism.

Anyhow, I passed my finals in the minimum time and started my career as a doctor.

But passing an examination is one thing, finding a subsequent job is another. While uncertain what to do, I noticed a great outcry in the newspapers about the shocking treatment of third-class emigrants on their way to America. I went to Liverpool and managed to get an appointment at £10 a month as a surgeon on board a tramp steamer called the *Palestine*. Strange to say, although the pay and accommodation were so poor on board such boats at that time, there were but few vacancies. Everyone preferred the interest and excitement of such jobs to the monotony of private practice. When I first saw the steamer after signing on, I thought I had signed my own death warrant. Anything was apparently considered good enough for the unfortunate emigrants. The ship had already been condemned as obsolete and discarded from its former service. The three hundred emigrants, married and single, were huddled together without any regard for decency or privacy. They were confined in two commodious holds that had been white washed, but that was about all that had been done in the way of preparations for them. There were no beds, only mattresses and some thin blankets that were quite insufficient as protection against the bitterly cold weather, for it was October. We encountered severe storms and it took us fifteen days to reach Boston, after spending three of them groping our way through an impenetrable fog off Newfoundland. The food was very bad and quite insufficient. When I told the Captain of the complaints I received on all sides about it, he became very indignant. I said that in my opinion it was not fit for dogs. After this heated quarrel, we hardly spoke to one another during the remainder of the voyage. He was, however, a magnificent seaman.

While the storms lasted, the hatches had to be battened down. The holds were badly ventilated and this added to the sufferings of the unfortunate emigrants. The atmosphere became stifling. I became seriously alarmed at the possibility of an outbreak of the dreaded ship-fever whose ravages were well remembered at that time. The wretched people sat huddled together in a pathetic attempt to give each other a little warmth. There was no proper nourishment for those who could eat but the majority were terribly seasick.

The return voyage took thirteen days and the sight of the sufferings of the poor animals that we now had as passengers was almost as depressing as the scenes witnessed on the outward voyage. The holds were now full of bullocks. It was almost impossible to walk the decks because of the sheds erected for the temporary accommodation of those for whom there was no room below. A few days later in a severe storm, they were all washed overboard and many of the cattle in the holds died from privation and disease.

This terrible voyage had a strange and dramatic aftermath for me many years afterwards. I had been particularly struck by the sufferings of one family among the emigrants on the way out, a family consisting of a father, mother and five or six little children, the oldest being a boy of about fifteen. I tipped the stewards as much as my limited means would allow to give them a little extra food. When they went ashore, as they were absolutely destitute, I borrowed a pound from a steward and gave it to them.

Years later when I was in practice in Cairo, I was attending some Americans occupying one of the best suites in Shepheards Hotel. The father's face seemed vaguely familiar but I could not remember for certain where I had met him before, if I had done so. One day he told me of the difficulties which his family had endured on their emigration to America. I discovered to my amazement that the prosperous American now before me was the half-starved boy of fifteen whose family I had assisted years before on the *Palestine*. I found that he now occupied an important position in a large and important business organization in the New World which enjoyed the unenviable reputation of having amassed its huge fortune by ruining multitudes of little men. Thinking of his own past, I asked him if these stories were true. He indignantly denied them but he did not give me the large cheque to help my work among the poor in Cairo which I felt my former services to his family merited. Even melodramatic meetings have their disappointments.

After that voyage, I felt that I had had enough of the sea, at least for the time being. So when I was offered the post of assistant to a doctor at Whalley in Lancashire at £70 per annum, I immediately accepted it. I believe that assistants in general practice now are paid as much as £400 a year with a generous allowance for their car. Things were very different then and a young doctor like myself felt himself lucky to get such an income. I was certainly paid for medical services rendered but I sometimes wonder why the modern assistant gets his magnificent salary. To judge from a case recently reported in the medical papers, purely medical work is at a discount compared to the mass of details which they have to compile for their panel practice. According to this report, an assistant broke his contract because excessive clerical work gave him writer's cramp and he was thus unable to obtain proper experience as a general practitioner.

I had little or no writing to do in my time. My "car" was a saddled horse and I carried my medical instruments in a black bag strapped to my back. Not an ideal way of paying professional visits but it had its compensations, although it was not always easy to gain the invalid's confidence and to make the required effort to do so when saturated with rain, snow or sleet. I doubt whether the modern panel patient who gets something for nothing all along the line would be altogether satisfied to see his doctor ride up on a spanking nag, or even in the traditional gig, with the historic black bag slung over his shoulders. These people want a man in a smart car who will prescribe them endless bottles of medicine. They would not appreciate the more intimate, human ways of the old days.

My work at Whalley was arduous on account of the long distances. Frequently I had to rise in the early hours of the morning, saddle a horse and ride several miles to a confinement. On arrival, sometimes wet through with rain or snow, I found conditions more than inadequate. The only light would be a bad foully smelling lamp. It was always difficult to obtain any hot water. As, even at that period, doctors were alternately praising and slandering Lister, I preferred to be on what I considered the safe side and insisted on boiling the instruments. This inevitably meant delay which at all costs should have been avoided in the interests of mother and child. In those days there were no ante-natal clinics, child welfare centres or spoon feeding of any sort and I very much doubt whether the sturdy, independent Lancashire folk of that period would have tolerated the meddlesome nonsense that is now talked and practised about such matters. In the lying-in-chambers in which I officiated in the eighties, instrumental interference was often urgent but anæsthesia had first to be induced without any assistance except from the loquacious "handy woman", the real Mother Gamp of fiction who was then always to be found in every cottage on these occasions.

When I hear of all the fuss that is made nowadays about what is, after all, merely a natural function, I can hardly suppress a smile. If the results were better than before, there might be some excuse for it, but I see no signs of there being less infection or anatomical injury. If medical students were properly trained, there would be no necessity for all this ante-natal paraphernalia. When I see doctors and nurses equipped with yashmaks (not always sterile by any means) and rubber gloves (likewise not always sterile), my feelings are very mixed. For one thing, I know that these rubber gloves interfere with the delicate sensitive touch—the *tactus eruditus*—of the great clinicians of the past. But the humorous side of the question tickles my fancy also. But then, I believe in the humoral theory of disease, first propounded by Hippocrates, the father of all medicine. Strangely enough his theories are becoming more and more popular in some quarters to-day, only about two thousand years since he propounded them.

I once attended two women on the same night in two villages miles apart from one another. There was a heavy storm and I had to ride through drenching rain on a jaded tired horse. But in spite of this and the rough attentions of the "handy woman", both mothers were out of bed in ten days. Much as I admired their courage and endurance, there seemed nothing strange or uncommon to me in their behaviour then. As a medical practitioner working among the poorer classes, I fully expected it. The unspectacular exhibiton of such qualities was my daily experience.

But now we are supposed to imagine that female courage is a new discovery. The feat of some woman aviator arouses hysterical outbursts of enthusiasm. It seems to be forgotten that the vast majority of women possess capacities for fortitude and endurance far greater than that required for flying. It is the aviators' mothers who should be considered the heroines in my opinion. As for their daughters, I am curious to know what their behaviour will be in face of natural ordeals but I doubt whether many details will be forthcoming.

A very curious custom existed in that Lancashire village and the surrounding districts. It throws much light on conditions then and now. If two young people liked each other and wished to marry, it was agreed that there should be a preliminary period during which they should "keep company". Then, if the girl gave practical proof of being able to produce offspring, they got married but not otherwise. The marriage tie was considered chiefly as an economic contract, based on the idea that the more children you had, the more wages would be the result for the whole family. For those were the good old days when there was no unemployment, and no dole, and when brewers, distillers, employers and owners of squalid insanitary property flourished and fattened. Much has changed for the better since then. On the other hand, in less than forty years, pernicious clinics have sprung up like mushrooms to limit or prevent childbirth. The conclusion may be drawn that morality and immoral practices are regulated and controlled, not by religious or ethical standards, but by the existing economic conditions.

And of all the changes that have taken place, none is to be more regretted than the passing away of the old country practitioner, and in fact of the old type of general practitioner everywhere. Some of the finest doctors and finest men that I have ever met were among the country practitioners of that period. They were endowed with sound common sense which they used every day in the exercise of their profession. This made them the trusted friends and advisers to their patients on many questions quite outside the province of medicine. If a family had some important problem to settle, they asked their doctor for his opinion as a matter of course. They knew that he would not abuse their trust and confidence.

Nowadays a doctor does not know his patients like this. They are usually so many cases to him, nothing more. He probably only sees them from time to time through a limited number of years. Then they move to another town or he himself goes elsewhere, and that is the end of his relations with them. Under these conditions, how can he get to know them as human beings? How can they think of him as a man on whom they can rely in the difficulties of their ordinary lives? It was quite different when the local practitioner had treated most members of a family, from the grandparents to the grandchildren. From the medical point of view alone, it had distinct advantages. Inherited diseases or inherited predisposition to a certain disease could be easily traced. Much valuable information is now lost by the lack of knowledge by any one doctor of a whole family's medical history. At the slightest provocation now, patients are sent to specialists who know even less of their background, and it is seldom much use for them to apply to the general practitioners for information. I have always noticed that every so-called advance in the practice of medicine has its disadvantages.

II

AFTER working for some months in Lancashire, I heard of a vacancy for a surgeon in one of the Elder Dempster West African steamers. I applied for the post, was accepted and so began my long association with the African Continent.

I was sent to Hamburg to join the ship, an old-fashioned craft of about 1,500 tons commanded by an irritable German who was much disliked by everyone. After a few days we steamed down the muddy Elbe in a terrific storm and had to shelter off Cuxhaven for a considerable time.

After a pretty rough passage in the North Sea and the Bay, we reached Madeira safely. I have never forgotten the beautiful scenery there. Then we went on to Santa Cruz, the capital of Tenerife. Here again the scenery was wonderfully fine. A snow capped peak rose several thousand feet above us, while we in the steamer were enjoying glorious sunshine in a bright blue sea. It was here that Nelson lost his arm and a flag taken from him during the siege is proudly shown to visitors in the Cathedral.

Shortly after leaving the Island, we encountered the trade winds that always blow in the same direction. Flying fish often landed on the deck. They are said only to be able to fly when their wings are wet. Eagles, looking like aeroplanes, were sometimes to be seen. The

sailors said that they were flying towards the West Indies.
One day I saw some small birds like those to be found in
great numbers near the Spanish coast in the Mediterranean. To my surprise, they were resting on the backs
of turtles. No one on board had ever seen such a sight
before and it aroused great excitement. As it was the
month in which the end of the world had been prophesied
by those strange people, the British Israelites, one of
whom happened to be a passenger on board, this curious
phenomenon made a great impression. But we were
more amused than otherwise by his assertion that it
proved the catastrophe to be near. It was not the first
time, nor the last, that I realized what a large number of
queer people there are in the world outside mental
hospitals.

At Cape Verde we had our first glimpse of Africa.
It looked very barren and desolate. Then we called at
Goree, a pestilential hole at that time never free from
Yellow Fever. Bathurst, the capital of Gambia, was much
better, nicely situated and fairly healthy. The Moslem
religion seemed to have made great headway there as in
all the Northern and Western parts of Africa. I came
across a society called the Sirra on one of my visits ashore
and found that it claimed to be one of the oldest, if not the
oldest, Mohammedan secret society in the world. There
were obvious signs of it having been influenced by
ancient Egypt. Legend said that the society was known
3000 B.C. It was a deeply mysterious organization claiming occult powers. Some of its passwords come from
such ancient languages that their meaning is now lost and
the officials themselves do not understand them.
Although it is mentioned in an Egyptian Papyrus dated

about 1600 B.C., some of its curious rites, such as that of circumcision, suggest that it originated among the negroes and their customs then spread to other countries.

Freetown, the capital of Sierra Leone, looked pleasant and attractive from a distance but disillusionment quickly followed on landing. The heat was terrible, the smells suffocating, and the lack of any adequate sanitary arrangements made life almost impossible for the Europeans. The natives were just beginning to adopt western modes and customs with curious results. The better class negroes had acquired a certain amount of education but it only seemed to make them insolent, aggressive and overbearing. Their womenfolk dressed in the latest frocks and hats from Paris but they fitted them so badly and were worn with so little regard for suitability and colour, their wearers looked more like caricatures than real people. In this semi-westernized mob, it was strange to meet native evangelists of the four square gospeller type. I saw one of them addressing a large crowd of natives on the Origin of Man. According to him, "God made Man from a piece of clay and stuck him on a fence to dry". He had just announced this with intense pious conviction when a member of his audience interrupted him with a shout, "Massa, who made dem fence?" For a moment the preacher seemed non-plussed, I thought that it was going to be too much for his elementary knowledge of theology, but then he replied in a severe tone: "Such interruptions very unseemly and enuf to upset any system of teology".

Some people say that they can distinguish between the various smells of Africa and recognize their origin.

This is certainly true of the African with his highly developed olfactory powers. Every tribe is said to have its particular odour which the natives themselves know immediately. On the other hand, they seem quite unaware of the appalling stenches that greet the visitor all along this pestilential coast. These foul smells cause intense suffering to the unfortunate whites condemned to live among them but the natives themselves seem to be quite oblivious of them. The primitive nose that can track an enemy by scent alone like a dog seems to have developed powers of self-protection unknown to the white man.

Native secret societies are said no longer to exist in Africa. They certainly did at the end of the last century. They were to be found everywhere, and of every kind— mystic, religious, protective, phallic, subversive, criminal, political and patriotic. Some of them were purely pagan, while others were Moslem and some a mixture of both.

These societies were conducted on systems very similar to those customary in civilized countries. They had their councils, supreme officials, grand masters, initiation ceremonies, passwords, signs and symbols. The basis of many of them was of a phallic nature, while others had mystic and religious rites. Circumcision and excision were largely practised all along the coast and took place after initiation to the Puberty Schools.

At Sierra Leone I came across the Poro, one of the greatest and most important of all the secret societies. Its name is invoked as a witness to covenants made between neighbouring tribes. When a native swears "By Poro", he will never break his oath, such is the dread of this terrible society among the common people. The

Poro has five signs and its members salute each other by bowing five times. The head of the order is called the Grand Tasso and his sign is called "dimonoi". It consists of a spiral of green palm or creeper and it hangs on the outer gate of the sacred enclosure. The Grand Tasso does not seem to have a very good time himself. He wears a mitre consisting of the skulls of his predecessors when he sits in council. On his selection and assumption of his office, he goes into strict privacy. He lives and dies alone. When he realizes that he is near his end, he crawls away into the bush to die. After a short interval the council meets and their first duty is to find the ant-cleaned skeleton. His skull is then added to the official mitre.

Among the many secret societies is one called the Tuntu which is reported to possess a potent medicine whose secret is carefully guarded. It is said to be able to counteract the effect of any poison, especially that placed on tabooed fishing nets.

The natives of Sierra Leone dedicate to their spirits places likely to inspire awe in the spectator, such as immensely large trees, huge rocks appearing in the midst of rivers or anything particularly strange or uncommon. This animistic tendency is to be found among most primitive races. Even among the American natives, any remarkable feature in natural scenery or dangerous places become objects of superstitious dread and veneration and are supposed to be the abode of gods. They believe that no death is natural or accidental but that the disease or accident by which it is immediately caused is the effect of some supernatural agency. In some cases they imagine that death is brought about by the malign agency of someone employing witchcraft against the deceased; in others, they think it has been inflicted by someone's tutelar demon in revenge for the deceased having practised incantations against his master. The sickness and death of chiefs and other people of consequence are usually attributed to the former cause, while that of the lower classes to the latter.

After Sierra Leone, our next port of call was Monrovia, the capital of the negro republic of Liberia. The fleet, consisting of one rotten-looking schooner, was lying at anchor in the harbour ready for any emergency. The American negro was to be seen here in his most objectional form, pompous, arrogant, dishonest and corrupt, and speaking with the most raucous nasal twang imaginable. He was frequently to be seen in full court dress, that is to say wearing a rather battered tall hat and a loin cloth. There seemed little real progress in Liberia, feuds between the various factions were frequent, slavery was winked at and although the country was rich in natural resources, there were many signs of terrible poverty among the people. Left to themselves, the native races were quickly reverting to their original barbaric state. The place was honeycombed with secret societies of every kind.

Further south is Grand Cess on the Kroo Coast. The "Kroo boys" are a very industrious and fairly intelligent people, capable of rising much higher in the social scale if properly taught and governed. At that time they did not seem to have much respect for the authorities at Monrovia. On our arrival, a gun was fired and hundreds of canoes made for the steamer, for the "Kroo boys" were much used then to do the heavy work on board for the white sailors. Each party of ten or twelve men had its own chief and foreman, the latter called by such a name as small rope, whisky and soda, flying fish or Gladstone. They were a fine body of men, hard working and good-humoured. A distinguishing tattoo mark ran from their foreheads to their noses and they also had their two centre teeth filed to sharp points. Their wages were paid in powder, old flint guns, salt, gaudy Manchester cotton goods and a peculiarly potent brand of gin which was so strong and vile that no white trader on the coast ever thought of touching it. Enormous quantities of this trade gin were discharged at every port and it was obviously in great demand among the natives. I have seen statues erected to men who posed as philanthropists and had yet become rich on this vile traffic, exchanging the gin for ivory, palm oil and kernels, rubber and other valuable commodities.

Accra and Cape Coast Castle, the chief towns on the Gold Coast, have always been important centres, but I could never understand why it is called the Gold Coast. In the old days of slavery, there must have been much traffic in gold but there were few signs of it when I was there. A secret society called the Dyora was much in evidence. It exercised a great influence over a large district and its rites were mainly phallic. At Accra I was fortunate enough to see a sort of Harvest Thanksgiving Festival. Thousands of people came from all directions to take part in it. There were innumerable processions, much dancing and drinking and the final orgy ended in a riot.

While out shooting at Accra, I had an accident that might have had serious consequences for me but for the intelligence of my little dog Snooks. I was standing near the edge of a high cliff when a bank of earth gave way. I fell headlong and should have crashed to the bottom if my fall had not been broken by a stunted tree growing out of the cliff side. I clung to it, but the cliff was far too steep for me to climb up it. Snooks at the top kept up a continuous howl for some time and then he suddenly ceased. There was no means of escape as far as I could see and the heat was terrific. After a couple of hours, I heard the dog barking again and this time joyously. To my delight and astonishment, she was not alone. Two sailors from the steamer were with her. Apparently she had returned to the ship and barked continuously until she had attracted attention. As I was missing, it was soon realized that something was wrong and the captain had sent two sailors to investigate. They soon rescued me by lowering some ropes but I really owed my escape from certain death to canine intelligence.

I noticed a tall wooden pillar here carved with phallic signs and a tortoise. On investigation, I found that it symbolized the Grand Egbo, the non-existent chief of a secret society bearing that name. Like many other secret societies, it was partly a philanthropic organization. Secrecy is apparently necessary for the practice of philanthropy in Africa, but charity covering a multitude of sins seemed to me to be nearer the truth.

We next anchored off Lagos, then the most important town on the coast. The bar was very shallow and dangerous and steamers had to anchor well out at sea. The place was infested with sharks. You could see them swimming round the ship accompanied by their small pilot fish.

On hearing that the great explorer Stanley was on board a steamer homeward bound then anchored near us, I thought it a good opportunity to pay him a visit, but I was not impressed either by his manners or his amiability. In fact, his taciturnity amounted to rudeness. On leaving I said: "Mr. Stanley, I have some excellent liver pills on my ship, may I have the honour of sending you some with directions?" He growled out an indignant reply and I beat a hasty retreat.

While here we were struck by a violent tornado. It was so terrific that it seemed as if the ship would capsize, by no means an inviting prospect in those shark infested waters.

Bonny is not far from Lagos. It was one of the most pestilential places on the whole coast, swarming with deadly mosquitoes. At that time continuous fighting was going on between the King Oko Jumbo and the native chiefs. The King and his sons wore European dress and were particularly European also in their love for alcohol. Slavery flourished and His Majesty was said to own thousands of slaves. They were considered a means of accumulating wealth but little value was placed on their lives. Because a slave had shot a parrot in a sacred tree held in great reverence by the natives, a terrible example was made to frighten the rest. The King gave orders for a general massacre and three hundred slaves were sacrificed in one day.

In various parts of Africa, the sacred Ju Ju tree is an object of great fear and veneration. The Ju Ju man frequently turns this fetish to good account. A British officer once saw a large crowd of natives standing round a sacred fig tree. It was a fine upright sapling but the

Ju Ju man had so hypnotized the mob that they thought it was a dead log lying flat on the ground. He then sprinkled blood on the bark and before the eyes of the astonished natives it stood erect, a position, however, from which it had never deviated for the British officer who witnessed the scene.

But these sacred trees are not actually worshipped. They are known locally as fetish trees through some peculiarity or abnormality in their growth and the various fetish objects of the tribe are hung in their branches.

Besides the mosquitoes that infested the almost endless swamps in the surrounding districts, there were man-eating tigers and ferocious gorillas in the jungle. The natives dared not venture out alone away from the villages. It was by no means an uncommon experience to return to such a place as Bonny after a few week's absence to find half the white men dead. The manner in which most of the traders lived certainly predisposed them to disease. They started drinking "gin and bitter" in the early morning and went on doing so with short intervals throughout the day. The enervating climate and the mosquito did the rest.

Another terrible pest ravaged these districts—driver ants. I saw them marching in columns twelve or fourteen abreast in the dense forests, but the first intimation of their presence had been sudden sharp bites on the legs. Monkeys, pigs and fowls are their usual prey, but they have been known to kill elephants. Of all animals the elephant is the least fitted to deal with a small enemy. Against a lion, leopard or man, it can use its crushing weight and pulverize an opponent with trunk and feet. But if attacked by the tiny driver ant, it can only flee into deep water or mud. There used to be a story of a British resident in West Africa who took a nap by the roadside on the way home from a party at a friend's house. In the morning a clean picked skeleton was found weirdly dressed in tropical clothes. The driver ants had found him while he slept and killed him before he could defend himself.

In every part of Africa that I visited, ants are to be seen in such overwhelming numbers that the question whether they will eventually prove a danger to mankind is not nearly so ridiculous as it may sound. The African ant is far from being the model creature suggested by Solomon. He has his vices. He is a slave trader and a nomad and resembles more the American bootlegger than a respectable member of society. The outstanding vice of the ant is drinking the sweet secretion of a particular type of beetle. They will go to any lengths to satisfy their craving for the precious liquor, even rescuing the grub of the insect in time of danger while neglecting the safety of their own offspring. Like mankind, they keep domestic servants and employ child labour. They wage war, using devices equivalent to all those known to man. And in one respect, they have an advantage over mankind. They are born perfect and fully developed ants when they emerge from the grub, and born with their vocation absolutely determined. For instance, an ant is born either to be a worker or a soldier. Then in both cases he is neuter in sex. When their nuptial flight has ended, the winged females remove their wings. Do they know that if it had not been for their wings, this climax in their lives would have been impossible? And do they know that they will never use them again? Even if they have this knowledge, why do they deliberately remove them? No one knows how the operation is actually performed and no scientist has ever offered a satisfactory explanation. But the poor females have been observed going down into holes in the ground and there in some way they take off their wings alone and unassisted by the workers. Nature has provided them with a weak transverse "fracture line" near the base of the wing but even then it is difficult to see how it can be snapped off so easily after the momentous flight. It looks like a profound act of renunciation of almost religious significance, as these females never see the light of day again. Henceforth they only produce eggs in an underground chamber.

The next important station at which we called was Old Calabar situated on one of the branches of the Niger a few miles from the sea. We went up the river for several miles. It was so narrow that the steamer was only a few feet from the bank on either side and almost brushed the trees. Nothing was to be seen but dense forest. Many beautiful birds, especially grey parrots, fluttered about in the branches keeping well out of reach of the innumerable monkeys. On every exposed piece of mud, a crocodile lay asleep. The trading station was nicely situated in a clearing and looked clean and prosperous. While going ashore in a small boat, Snooks who was playing on the main deck saw me and immediately plunged into the river. Without thinking, I plunged in too and we were both rescued just in time as an enormous crocodile swam towards us. A short time afterwards a small boy playing on one of the wharves fell into the river and was seized by one of these savage brutes before he could be rescued.

43

At the back of the station, you quickly got into a pleasant country of woods, hills and valleys that afforded a variety of shooting. One day having ventured too far accompanied only by Snooks, I came across about twenty naked savages. Most of the tribes in this district were cannibals and the knowledge hardly increased my peace of mind. They wore feathers in their hair but otherwise they were quite naked. They rushed towards me all shouting and continued making a tremendous noise for about fifteen minutes. I imagined that they were discussing whether to eat me or not. Then a flock of wild turkeys flew over our heads. With some trepidation I fired at them and fortunately brought one of them down. The natives seemed considerably impressed but they went on shouting and finally one of them struck Snooks with his spear. This was too much for me and I covered the man with my rifle. On this, the others bolted leaving the offending savage so terror stricken that he seemed unable to move. I disarmed him and let him go, and then returned as quickly as possible to the village.

While at Old Calabar, a royal canoe arrived asking for medical assistance. It appeared that a powerful king living about twenty miles up the river was ill and required a doctor at once. After obtaining permission from the captain, I left at once in that wonderful canoe. There were forty boys paddling on either side. I sat under a large sunshade in the stern. All the boys paddled in unison while a sort of jazz band played the whole time.

I found His Majesty suffering from a curable malady and I was able to give him immediate relief. As a fee for my services, I received a puncheon of Palm oil then worth about twenty-eight pounds.

44

Late on the following day I was invited to visit His Majesty and stay the evening. I found the patient much better. He made me a very tempting offer to stay with him permanently as his official doctor. Afraid of offending him by an immediate refusal, I managed to defer a final decision until later. Meanwhile I was made a blood brother of some secret society, the Egbo or one of its affiliations. I was initiated into the mysteries that constitute brotherhood with the tribe. The ceremony was accompanied by much ritual. The bark of some tree saturated with aromatic herbs was burnt causing clouds of smoke and a sweet rather sickly smell. Strange noises emanated from the Council House. I was told that the spirits were being consulted. Weird barbaric music was played. It was rather like a spiritualistic séance in some Mayfair drawing-room. The approval or disapproval of the spirits apparently depended on the tone of the voices of the priests, for ventriloquism obviously played a very important part in the ceremony. The head man wore a dreadful-looking mask and the other officials most imposing regalia. When at last it was all over and I had been accepted as a blood brother of the tribe, a sumptuous banquet was served with the inevitable but delicious palm oil chop, followed by a dance. An enormous quantity of trade gin was consumed. I had never witnessed an African orgy before and I was hardly prepared for the indescribable licentiousness of the proceedings. Snooks shivered violently the whole evening and at times I felt rather sick myself. The dancing was certainly wonderful, especially the snake dancing, but besides all the turmoil of the dancers, a drum was beaten the whole time and I found it a most disturbing, nerve-racking

45

sound. It spoke a language of its own well understood by the natives. Like the voices of the spirits as interpreted by the priests, it sometimes expressed disapproval, sometimes entreaty in the most haunting and mysterious way. No one who has once heard an African drum in the bush can ever forget it.

Most of the natives were cannibals but physically they were fine specimens of humanity. They were very brave and had a high code of honour, prizing virtue in their women above all things. Divorce was completely unknown among them, adultery was a penal offence for which death was the usual punishment.

In every village in West Africa there is a Joss House containing a sacred image. They vary from large thatched houses to squalid-looking hovels. The more elaborate constructions are decorated with the skulls of defeated enemies, but empty gin bottles serve the same purpose on the poorer houses.

In spite of differences of interpretation, the fundamental beliefs and dogmas of the natives are the same right through pagan Africa, with one notable exception. There is one sect that worships Satan. It is to be found mostly in the Cameroons and the Belgian Congo. They believe that manual labour of any kind is a sin and thus come into frequent conflict with the white settlers. Their initiation ceremony includes signing a pact with the Devil in their own blood. Horrible crimes are attributed to them, such as infanticide before baptism, incest and the murder of young children so as to obtain a magic ointment from their bodies.

I came across many instances of witchcraft. The wizard of the tribe is a very important man, for everyone believes that he can put a spell on crops, cattle or even the weather, in fact on practically everything that conduces to human happiness. It is thus not surprising that the wizard, witch doctor or Ju Ju man wields great power and is much feared.

The African native thinks nothing so suitable for Voodoo or magic as the body of a white person, especially a woman, but curiously enough the body of a dead gorilla is considered quite as good. An ointment is prepared from the dead body and this is used for Voodoo. The graves of white men are often ravaged for this purpose. A Belgian official in the Kwanga Province of the Belgian Congo was once murdered solely because the witch doctor leading a rebel movement wanted his head. Every village of any importance in the Kalamba region received a portion of the body to use in the making of magic amulets.

The ceremonies that took place at night were very like the Sabbat or nocturnal fetes of the Middle Ages. I attended one of these orgies in the Cameroons. There was the usual banquet followed by licentious dancing, accompanied by Tom Tom music and the firing of guns. A witch doctor presided over the whole revolting performance at which the new initiates were smeared with some magic ointment.

The Cameroons at this period belonged to Germany and differed in many respects from the other parts of Africa that we had visited. Instead of the low dreary monotonous coast along which we had been drifting, there was a fine open country, well wooded, with snow-capped mountains rising in the distance. The Germans were obviously very unpopular with the natives and the country was in a most disturbed state. A German gun-boat that lay at anchor in the river had been in action on the previous day. As a result, some teutonic skulls must have been added to the construction of some Joss Houses in the neighbourhood. And yet it has been my experience that cannibal tribes are quiet, inoffensive people if left alone. Their moral code and respect for their women folk is often far superior to that of their neighbours. As a rule a cannibal is brave, a great hunter, reliable and a hard worker. He seldom has any slaves. His domestic life is very correct and from the sexual point of view he is very chaste. He may thus be con-sidered in many respects a shining example to many so-called civilized peoples whose newspapers are full of their infidelities. The whole question of the eating of human flesh hinges on the totem pole, known as *tanne* in the language of many primitive tribes. The totem is the hereditary emblem of a tribe or clan from which they take their name. It symbolizes to these people a mythical ancestor generally an animal. Each tribe believes that it is descended from a lion, elephant, tiger or some other beast. The tribesman is thus forbidden to eat the animal symbolizing his own tribe, but he can of course dine on the people of another tribe because they are descended from another animal. He would be horrified if he realized that he had eaten a fellow man, that is to say a man descended from the same animal as himself. But according to his idea of the totem, there is nothing whatsoever to get excited about in eating a man from a neighbouring tribe. It is like eating a pheasant from your neighbour's preserves.

A French traveller in the Congo recently described how

his porters who were very hungry captured a large tortoise one day. Unhappily one of them believed that he was descended from a tortoise and for some time he refused to take part in the meal. But finally his hunger and the exhortations of his fellows overcame his reluctance. After the meal, however, he became so terrified at what he had done that he was violently ill. He was convinced that he had eaten his own ancestors.

The belief of the Sierra of the Ivory Coast is quite typical. The natives believe that on a man's death his soul passes into an animal of his totem. They thus regard the killing and eating of such an animal with extreme horror, since it would mean that they were consuming a late member of their tribe.

The totem poles are usually made from great tree trunks carved from top to bottom with the figures of animals and men, surmounted by the figure of a porpoise, eagle, raven, wolf, bear or sometimes that of the man or woman whose ashes are contained in a cavity in the pole. The figures of the animals or birds represent the guardian spirit of each particular clan or tribe.

From the Cameroons, we went on to Fernando Po. It was an extremely pleasant trip. We were now not far from the equator and the heat was suffocating, but all along the coast we could see long ranges of snow-capped mountains. We passed enormous spouting whales and other large fish. But in the midst of all this variety of scenery and animal life, my main thought was what kind of people inhabited those mountains and the country beyond, then the least known part of Africa. Except that the presence of innumerable gorillas and elephants has

49

been proved by explorers, I doubt whether much more is known about it to-day.

Fernando Po, a Spanish settlement, is a beautiful island standing out fresh and green in the scorching sunlight. The land rises gradually from the sea shore to the interior where it reaches a considerable height, all covered with the most luxurious vegetation. The slopes of the hills are so well wooded that it looks like an island of forests. While at anchor in the bay I saw an extraordinary and most uncommon sight: a fight between a sword fish, a whale and a thresher. The whale put up no fight at all. It remained motionless while the sword fish stabbed him again and again with his formidable weapon, while the thresher hammered away on the whale's back with tentacles that looked exactly like the flail used in threshing corn. This unequal combat continued for hours. The water all round became red with blood.

It was so tantalizing not to be able to follow the combat in detail that I persuaded the captain to allow me to launch a dinghy with two sailors. On reaching the scene of battle, I could see nothing except the tentacles of the thresher. The whale seemed to be moribund but it was impossible to ascertain the exact condition of the combatants. After consulting with the sailors, I decided to land on the whale. So accompanied by Snooks, I climbed on to its back that was dry and blistered by the sun. It was an enormous creature but I had no time to take any measurements, as quite suddenly a number of sharks were seen obviously greatly agitated, for they were lashing the sea with their tails. The sailors were terribly frightened and for a moment I thought that I was going to be marooned and deserted by them. They stood by, however, but it was quite impossible for me to return to the dinghy, the position was too critical. Whether it was the sight of us or the blood on the surrounding waters, I do not know, but something had terribly excited these appalling monsters. My first thought was for my dog. Seizing a favourable opportunity, I threw her into the arms of one of the sailors who had difficulty in holding her as she struggled violently to return to the whale.

My position was now very precarious. To add to my terrors, I thought the monster was beginning to submerge. So I resolved to act, and to act quickly. Fortunately the whale was not slippery, either because its skin had been dried by the heat of the sun or more probably because it had lost so much blood. All around me I could see innumerable sharks and strange fish, lashing themselves into a fury in the blood tinged waters. There was one shark that especially attracted my attention. He appeared to be the leader. His movements were terrifying. At one moment he swam rapidly as if making for an imaginary enemy, then he turned over on his back with his mouth open, lashing his tail furiously, before plunging into the depths to rise later to the surface and repeat the performance. Rifle in hand, I carefully watched his movements, feeling that my safety depended on my immediate action. At last I saw a favourable opportunity; I fired and the ball entered his head. There was a terrible commotion and for a moment it was impossible to say what had happened. All the other sharks crowded round like the mob rushing to offer unwelcome assistance at a street accident. Fortunately for me the crowd were all mourners on this occasion. Taking advantage of the situation, I fired again with the same satisfactory result. All this time, the dinghy had remained close at hand watching events and when I had established peace with my rifle, the sailors returned and rescued me from the water.

On the way back to the steamer, I saw many sharks' fins protruding from the waves but we were not molested in any way. Those on board had been watching our movements but no one had had the slightest idea of what was really happening or assistance would have been sent. In fact, I soon realized that my story was barely believed and I seldom alluded to it during the passage. I never mentioned that at one time I had thought of imitating Jonah and seeking refuge in the whale's mouth that protruded above the waves. But when the writer of the fable of Jonah and the whales writes about the prophet being swallowed, he was clearly no naturalist, although there is certainly room for many men in an ordinary whale's mouth, which may well measure twenty feet long, fifteen feet high and nine feet wide. I could certainly have secured a temporary refuge in the monster's mouth if the sharks had not taken it into their heads to follow me. But I feel sure that my reputation for veracity would then have been completely destroyed if I had ever dared to tell the story. The feat, however, has actually been accomplished. On October 14th, 1771, an Edgartun whaling vessel struck a whale which then bit in two one of her boats. Marshall Jenkins, a member of the crew, was washed into the whale's mouth and sunk with it as it dived. On returning to the surface, the whale ejected him on to the wreckage of the broken boat, much bruised but not seriously injured. The striking event was recently mentioned by Sir John Bland Sutton in the *British Medical Journal*.

Our next port of call was Gaboon where there is a fine harbour. I was very interested to hear about the animal life abounding in the district, especially the gorillas. The strange doctrine of evolution was far more popular and more widely accepted at that time than it is to-day. Being interested in the subject like every doctor or scientist of the period, I made a close study of the gorillas and the local tribes, the powerful Mangoes and Fans, but I could find no resemblance whatsoever between them.

The gorillas are strict vegetarians, living on nuts and a kind of wild onion of which they are very fond; the native tribes are all cannibals and therefore carnivorous. Then matricide and patricide are practically unknown among the gorillas, although some very old ones are occasionally found living alone, as if they have been ostracized by their younger fellows. Far worse conditions prevail among the natives tribes. It was by no means uncommon for old women to be thrown into the river to be eaten by the crocodiles. The crime was carried out in a perfectly legal manner. First of all, the priests of the local Joss House examined the case and gave their permission. A procession would then be formed and on arrival at the nearest river or lake, the old woman would be thrown headlong into the river, perhaps by her son. Sometimes she might make a brave effort to escape by swimming but the crocodiles, used to being fed in this manner, would soon end the sufferings of the poor victim. Meanwhile, those who had accompanied her to the fatal spot had immediately returned to the village without ever looking back to see what had happened.

The same sort of ghastly procession took place during the protracted illness of a king or powerful chief. Frequently a young girl would be accused of having bewitched him and she would be dispatched in this manner, one more skull being added to the Joss House. Unfortunately it did not always end with one; victim after victim was required until the patient fully recovered.

Such native customs form an unpleasant contrast to the strong family life of the gorillas, who would never think of behaving in this manner. Family ties are always preserved with them and in some respects they seem to have a higher standard of social life than primitive human beings, and even those claiming to be fully civilized. For the gorilla cannot endure the gramophone and jazz, while he responds immediately to better kinds of music. Although a comparatively small matter, this difference of taste between gorillas and human beings hardly supports the theory of evolution.

We next called at Boma at the entrance of the magnificent Congo river. While anchored here, a most distressing accident occurred. Two sailors were engaged in painting the side of the vessel and the platform on which they were seated suddenly gave way. They fell headlong into the rapidly flowing river. They seemed unable to grasp the various objects that were immediately thrown into the water in the hope of effecting a rescue. It seemed as if some invisible force was dragging them down and that they were powerless to resist it. They must have been seized by the ground sharks known to infest these waters. The whole scene was over in less than a minute. The terrible fate of the poor fellows cast a gloom over the steamer. Much sympathy was felt for their relations in Liverpool, poor struggling people who depended on the miserable wages paid at that period which automatically ceased at the sailors' deaths. As no workmen's compensation act existed at that time, nothing could be done.

We next touched at St. Paul de Loanda, the capital of Angola, a Portuguese settlement. In spite of the fine harbour, the town itself gave an impression of decay. It seemed deserted and nothing is so depressing as a place where people once lived and prospered but which they have now left. Loanda was formerly a great slave depot and it still showed evidence of the ghastly traffic. The inhabitants seemed to be of a very low type, wallowing in filth and depravity.

While we were there, a remarkable company of strolling artistes appeared in the town. They numbered about thirty and were all under four feet in height. They were without exception perfectly formed and seemed extremely healthy. They had no rickets, tuberculosis or other maladies that so often give rise to distinctive deformities, such as achondroplasia. Fair in colouring, they were unusually intelligent for natives. An air of mystery surrounded them that could not be penetrated as their language was unknown to any of the local tribes. On the other hand, they could obviously comprehend what was going on around them.

They gave a performance in the open air which somewhat resembled that of the Picola Comedians in Italy or the mechanical feats executed by marionettes. Their arrow shooting was amazing. They loosed one arrow and another shortly afterwards. The second, travelling at the faster rate, stuck into the end of the first one in the air. Then they shot an arrow at a man's head and it appeared to penetrate both cheeks, the point sticking out on one side and the feathered end on the other. As dancers, they appeared to have every muscle under complete control. First one muscle began to move, then another, until all the muscles co-ordinated and produced the desired effect, the sensuous naturally predominating.

To all appearances as light as an india-rubber ball, one of them alighted on a banana leaf and danced on it without causing it to move in the slightest.

No one could tell me who these remarkable little people really were. They made their appearances at the coastal ports quite suddenly and as suddenly disappeared, always surrounded with the same impenetrable mystery. I tried to discover from what part of Africa this race of pygmies came but without success. They were energetic, hardy people, temperamental and humorous, very far from the doomed race of degenerates so often depicted by travellers. In my opinion, the communities of pygmies known to exist in central Africa must be survivals from some very ancient race. They have a much higher level of intelligence than the average native, and although some travellers have stigmatized them as cowardly, there does not seem to be much justification for the reproach. A recent traveller, Commander Gatti, speaks highly of the invaluable assistance which they gave him as guides. In the green inferno of the impenetrable forest, you soon lose all sense of direction. Without the help of the pygmies, he would have completely lost his way and eventually died of hunger and thirst. But the little men, shy and silent, never left him for one moment and guided him without the slightest hesitation through their mysterious forest kingdom, finding the least difficult routes, opening from time to time a passage for him with their machetes and taking advantage of the tracks of their implacable enemies, the Ngagi or gorillas.

The best account that has ever appeared concerning these interesting people is in the book written by Père R. P. Trilles, now of the Catholic Institute of Paris. Père Trilles is well known as a conscientious observer. He has lived for years in the equatorial forest in the midst of these little people, sharing their hardships and little by little gaining their confidence. He also learned their language, and of course you cannot really get to know a people unless you understand what they say. He was thus able very gradually to penetrate mysteries hitherto rigorously concealed from all strangers. He witnessed ceremonies never before seen by a white man. According to him, the pygmies have magicians who obtain such extraordinary results by their magic that they would seem unbelievable to anyone who does not accept occult forces among the primitive tribes. Père Trilles examines these little people from every aspect, including their physical, religious, social and moral lives. He states in conclusion that although isolated from other tribes and hunted by them for centuries, they have qualities all their own. They have developed certain senses, such as sight, touch, smell and orientation, to an extent far beyond that of the other tribes in Africa. But more extraordinary still are their preter-natural powers which exceed that of any of the other primitive tribes.

That these little people, living from hand to mouth in the depths of the forests surrounded by enemies, should unaided have developed a social system founded on religious principles and possess as well a profound practical knowledge of the unknown occult powers, is one of the greatest mysteries of darkest Africa.

The African dwarf is not deformed in any way, he is simply a fully developed man in miniature. In most other countries, it is rare to find a dwarf without deformity, as is proved by the artists of the past in their pictures. For instance, in the famous picture of "The Coronation of Cosmo de Medici", there are several dwarfs wearing court dress and they all have enormous heads. Then the dwarf in "The Triumph of Julius Cæsar" is a fine example of scrofula and rickets with an obvious disorganization of the glands of internal secretion. There is a typical dwarf in the "Club Foot" by Libera in the Louvre who shows all the indications of infantile paralysis. "The Dwarf" by Sebastian de Morra is a good example of achondroplasia. In the Cairo Museum there is also a statue of a person called Pet-Pess-Nesu suffering from hydrocephalus. It belongs to the old Kingdom 3000 B.C. Elephantiasis is depicted in the state of King Menthuhopte, 2000 B.C. While on the walls of the tombs at Beni Hassan are several pictures of men suffering from rickets.

The pygmies of central Africa are thus all the more remarkable since their miniature size is not accompanied by any obvious deformity or disease.

I have often wondered why dwarfs were such favourite subjects for artists in Latin countries, especially as it was and still is the custom to cross the fingers on seeing one, to avert the evil eye. Swallowing three times was also considered a good remedy. I have seen Italians talking to hunchbacks or other deformed persons with fingers crossed, their hands behind their backs.

After St. Paul de Loanda, we turned homewards calling at various ports for passengers and cargo. We stopped off the Kroo coast to enable the "boys" to go ashore and return to their villages. Their disembarkation was a strange sight. Frequently, if the canoes did not arrive quickly enough, the captains of the steamers got impatient and their luggage was hurled overboard. It was carefully packed in boxes, including their wages of trade gin, and it did not seem to suffer any harm. We were several miles from the shore but the Kroo boys thought nothing of swimming the whole way pushing their luggage in front of them, in spite of the sharks known to infest these waters.

Passing through the Bight of Benin, we saw large numbers of whales disporting themselves in the warm water. At some of the stations, we found that some of the white traders whom we had seen only a few weeks before apparently in good health were now dead. Gin and the anopheles had effectively done their work. Except among the witch doctors, the mosquito was supposed to be remotely connected with malaria. I have no doubt that many valuable lives could have been saved had appropriate treatment been administered. Far too much reliance was placed on quinine as a prophylactic. Shortly after leaving Cape Coast Castle, practically everyone on board the steamer, both passengers and crew, was ill with malaria or dysentery. The captain and all the officers and engineers except three were ill. Two stewards who fortunately remained well had to look after over sixty sick people. Owing to the serious shortage of officers, I had to keep watch on the bridge. One night I thought I heard a slight thud and a shout from the sea. The atmosphere was quite clear as it always is in these latitudes and we could not understand what had happened. A collision seemed out of the question. The engines were soon stopped and a boat was lowered to find out what had happened. Then two amphibious natives were seen swimming rapidly towards the steamer. We had run down a fishing boat carrying no lights. The two men were soon rescued, two stalwart negroes who had been the whole crew.

The incident hardly reflected on my seamanship but I found the story very useful in cheering up my patients. Some of them laughed so heartily at the doctor's account of the collision that they immediately began to get better. Others who were more or less delirious during the night would not believe that anything serious had happened until the two rescued natives were shown to them. This had the desired result and all my patients made a good recovery except one, an officer in a West Indian Regiment, who died of dysentery some days after leaving the African coast. It is a curious fact that many cases of malaria or dysentery either developed or became worse in the regions of the trade winds on the homeward voyage.

The case of the officer made a profound impression on me at the time. I felt, and still do feel, that he should not have died. I can see even now his widow waiting for him on the landing stage at Liverpool, for there was no wireless in those days and the first intimation which she received of her husband's death was on the arrival of the steamer. It is strange how some deaths make an impression on a doctor and others do not. That was only one in my long career, and yet it stands out in my mind as a pathetic tragedy. It is not that I was in any way responsible myself, I merely followed the erroneous medical teaching of the period.

Looking back now and calmly studying the teaching then in vogue concerning dysentery, it is difficult to understand how it could have been sanctioned, approved and practised by renowned physicians with international reputations. They were not only wrong in principle; their methods were against all reason, common sense and the laws of nature. The importance of watching natural developments and avoiding all needless interference strongly impressed itself on me early in my medical career on the West African Coast, where there were many opportunities of observing disease in its gravest forms. But this theory, while undoubtedly advantageous to the patient, is not always so to the physician's reputation. The patient himself and his friends seldom have any use for masterly inactivity. They expect the continual administration of drugs, serums and vaccines, the newest inventions and discoveries always commanding the greatest amount of confidence and respect. Now the administration of remedies, if judiciously applied, may assist nature, but as often as not it interferes with the patient's chance of recovery. Disease, after all, is but a variation from the normal, and like all natural variations it tends to revert to the normal if left to the wonderful healing power of nature itself.

After the collision with the native craft, the unfortunate officer on the bridge with me, so ill that he could hardly keep his feet, again set the course. I ventured to suggest that if such a course were followed, it would land us in trouble. My prediction was almost fulfilled. I took the precaution of using the lead and steaming at less than half speed. I was on the point of giving the order to reverse when the watch reported breakers ahead. It was a terrible moment. In an instant the engines were reversed but an ominous thud was felt and the steamer appeared to stand still for some minutes. Meanwhile the engines were working full speed astern, churning up the water on either side with great force. At last a little movement was felt, then another, and finally a distinct jerk which meant deep water and the saving of nearly a hundred lives from a horrible death.

Many steamers and sailing vessels used to run ashore on the inhospitable African coast where lights were few and far between in those days. When such accidents happened, the result was often disastrous. I heard of shipwrecked crews who were never heard of again and may well have been killed and eaten by the natives. Immediately a ship struck, thousands of natives would approach from all directions, shouting and screaming and mad with lust for plunder. When the gin and rum were discovered, terrible scenes ensued. Fortunately for the crew, the natives sometimes became so drunk that they allowed them to escape unharmed.

Sailors were miserably paid in those days, seldom more than a few pounds a month, but they were allowed to do some personal trading with the natives, obtaining such live commodities as monkeys, parrots and birds. The fo'c'sle was a foul hole at the best of times; you had to go down a ladder into a badly ventilated and ill-lighted compartment surrounded by bunks. In bad weather when the port holes had to be kept closed, the air became stifling, hardly improved by the presence of parrots and monkeys which the sailors had collected from the natives. Rats also abounded. I have known them to be so numerous and vicious on board a West African steamer that a guard had to be placed over a sick sailor to protect him from them.

While the sailors were living under these appalling conditions, the shipowners in Liverpool could be seen rigged out in their best black clothes after service on Sunday, sanctimoniously masquerading as men of position and wealth. There was another side of the picture that was hardly complimentary to them and their ideas of religion.

Quite apart from the sailors and their miserable lives on trading steamers, I think that there are thousands of miles along the West Coast of Africa unfit for any white man to live in for any length of time. As for a white woman, it is what the Americans would call mental cruelty to ask her to reside anywhere on the coast at all. The moist enervating climate with its high temperature and heavy winds, the appalling stenches, the bad water supply, the terrible monotony, the constant association with negroes of low mentality, all combined with the inevitable malaria to undermine the health and constitution of any white settler. No one could live on the coast at the time of which I write without his character and disposition being seriously modified for the worse. I only heard of one man then, a doctor, living the regulation twenty years—half of which were spent in Europe—to qualify for his well-earned pension. Sooner or later, the Coast Dyscrasia manifested itself with the unmistakable sallow complexion which was always a forerunner of an early death.

Of course in the matter of treatment and diagnosis, many advances have been made with regard to tropical diseases of recent years; but I do not believe that it is possible to convert any station along the West African Coast into a sufficiently healthy place for Europeans to live in without running serious dangers. It seems incredible but not so very long ago physicians were prejudiced against the use of water either internally or externally in fever cases. I have seen patients suffering from typhus, typhoid, malaria and dysentery, simply dying of thirst and insufficient nourishment. I have always believed myself in the curative effect of plain water, even as a student when such a belief was looked upon with considerable disfavour. I have never lost faith in the efficacy of water, nature's own remedy. Many bottles of medicine would do just as much good if they contained nothing else.

I was much impressed on that voyage by the terrible nature of the trading conditions. Deadly weapons and even more deadly drink were bartered for valuable commodities. If anyone doubts the immorality of this traffic, they should have attended one of the nightly orgies in any of the native villages. These ceremonies were the direct result of providing primitive savages with liquor. Demoralizing scenes took place and bestial crimes were committed. The truth about them has probably never been told, simply because no white man ever dared to remain to see the climax to the preliminary scenes of drunkenness and debauchery.

On the other hand, the savage tribes seem to have

retained certain primitive accomplishments which more civilized races have lost. For instance, they undoubtedly have a system of telepathy between one another which no longer exists among European peoples. They believe, and are justified in their belief, that persons and things at a distance can exert sympathetic influences over other people. The West African native certainly can perform many wonders which the white man is far too inclined to classify as magic without attempting to understand or to analyse further. Hypnotism (practised in the Puberty Schools), exorcism based on suggestion, clairvoyance and telepathy have been developed to an extraordinary extent among these tribes and probably form the basis of their so-called magic, although the transference of thought from one individual to another is denied by many scientists with great reputations. I know that they can throw a medium into a cataleptic trance which lasts for several days during which the subject is entirely insensible to pain. The witch doctor is very proficient in the use of these natural or preter-natural forces and can effect cures which the orthodox doctor is powerless to achieve. He also understands the properties of drugs unknown to us in Europe. This is especially the truth with regard to poisons. There is one in particular which leaves no visible trace in the body and has no apparent effect and yet inevitably causes death after a time. They are said to extract poisons from snakes and to use them with deadly effect when it suits their purpose.

The fact that mosquitoes cause malaria was known to them a long time ago. More extraordinary still is the fact that they knew the malaria virus to be a cure or rather palliative for general paralysis many years before it was discovered by European doctors. We have only recently begun to use this treatment, but for centuries the natives were in the habit of sending such cases to malaria districts to be bitten by mosquitoes.

I came across instances of negroes let loose on the West African Coast finding their way back to their own homes simply by the sense of smell. Or is it a sixth sense? Butt Thompson says that in mixed assemblies they can detect their own tribal odour even when blindfolded and that they can single out the members of their own family from a village gathering without looking at them. The universal savage mode of greeting by smelling or sniffing (usually alluded to as rubbing noses) must obviously be connected with the same phenomenon, as well as the notorious smelling out of suspected persons by witchcraft. We know that animals make use of their sense of smell in their recognition of their kith and kin, friends or foes and for other purposes. Here we have the same sense highly developed amongst savage people, and we have to confess that we know very little about it.

It is also surprising to discover that primitive man has a system of dietetics based on sound physiological principles in spite of the variety of his customs and habits. It is a universal belief among these natives that such qualities as strength, virility, speed of movement, courage, timidity, stupidity, lethargy, can all be acquired by assimilating the flesh, blood and organs of persons and animals possessed of them when alive. The lion's flesh is eaten and his blood drunk in order to acquire courage and strength. On the other hand, natives will not eat hares for fear of being affected by this animal's timidity. On the same principle, lethargic people are given a diet of ants and a stupid man is said to have the flesh or the brains of an hyena. The young Dynkas will not eat venison because they believe that it would make them timid, while the Red Indians will not eat any flesh of coarse gross quality as they rightly consider that dullness of mind would be the result.

In some places men eat the heart, tongue, liver and testicles of their slain enemies, believing that in these parts the soul resides, while a New Zealand chief would eat the eyes of his dead enemy in the belief that it would improve his own sight. In Uganda, the liver is regarded as the seat of the soul and it is eaten with the express purpose of improving all one's powers. There is thus nothing new in the frightful concoctions now being made by enterprising manufacturing chemists and guaranteed to effect remarkable cures of revitalization.

The despised pig does not appear to be endowed with any peculiar properties among savages and there is nothing comparable to its popularity among civilized people.

These dietetic theories of the natives are doubtless the meaning and origin of cannibalism. What can be more natural after a hard fought battle among savages than for the victor to dine off his fallen foe, if he believes that he is thus invigorated and his courage strengthened? No doubt the prospect of another sumptuous feast increases his lust for battle.

Then they believe that any bean or vegetable resembling any part of the human body possess the virtues of that part. In view of what is usually regarded as our recently acquired knowledge of the ductless glands, the fact that in primitive science each part of a man's body

67

was thought to be impregnated with certain virtues is of special interest. This, of course, also applied to the bodies of animals in their conception. Clothed in scientific verbiage, we are now asked to believe that certain products extracted from glands of animals contain important properties that stimulate heart and muscles. The savage knew all this thousands of years ago, and he also knew that the surest way of benefiting from these glands was to eat them in their raw state and to eat them whole. There is much which modern medicine could learn from a study of these primitive peoples. For one thing, it would show some scientists that some of their discoveries are not quite so original as they imagine.

III

DURING my last voyage to West Africa, I met Dr. E. P. Philpots, Managing Director of Monte Dore and proprietor of Bourne Hall, Bournemouth, who was a passenger on his way to the Canary Islands. He advised me to give up sea-faring and invited me to stay with him on my return from Africa which I did.

Dr. Philpots was a very accomplished, much travelled and versatile man. Amongst other wanderings, he had acted as surgeon to an Arctic Expedition and his breezy manner and continual cheerfulness must have done much to brighten the lives of its members in the desolate regions of the North. Bournemouth even then was remarkable for the order and cleanliness observed everywhere, and also for the myriads of elderly people, mostly women, either in bath chairs or aimlessly walking in the streets, all wearing respirators. These strange contrivances have now been discarded, only to be replaced, however, by every kind of fur and woollen garment. Even children are still enveloped in tight fitting woollen garments "to keep the cold out". The germ of the common cold has an easy time of it when people do this sort of thing.

After a short stay at Bourne Hall, I was asked to become private physician to a General then living in a large house in Parkstone. He had spent nearly all his life in India and Burmah and was a very remarkable man. When in a good humour, he told me about his interesting experiences abroad, but he was not always in an amiable mood and then I had to prescribe riding or hunting which were the best medicines for him. We used to go long distances, sending the horses to some place in the surrounding district the night before. On one occasion I nearly lost my life. I tried to jump a swollen stream when the bank gave way beneath the horse's feet and we both fell into the water. I had to wade about four hundred yards with the water up to my neck before I succeeded in getting the horse on to dry land again. Then, soaked to the skin, we had to return to Parkstone which was fully twelve miles away. I was none the worse for the adventure but the poor horse took a long time to recover. On my arrival in the early hours of the morning. I found the General greatly agitated. He had heard most alarming rumours of the disaster and was thus so agreeably surprised to see me that a marked improvement in his condition was the result. Another incident of a more amusing character occurred shortly afterwards, which also contributed towards his recovery.

In the house where we were staying, there were two ladies who considered themselves too ill ever to leave their beds. One of them certainly looked the picture of health and was "fat, fair and forty". Everything was tried in the attempt to persuade her to leave her bed but without success, although she was heard surreptitiously walking about her room during the night. One morning I visited her and said: "Miss Jones, I want you to get out of bed." She replied with her usual obstinate refusal. "Very well, Miss Jones," I said, "if you won't get up, I shall get into bed with you." And I proceeded to take off my coat. When I had got as far as hanging it over the back of a chair, Miss Jones jumped out of bed screaming. I picked up my discarded garment and unconcernedly left the room, only to fall helplessly on the floor convulsed with the laughter in the General's room downstairs. When I told him what had happened, his merriment was quite uncontrollable. He seriously suggested that I should try the same cure on the other lady, but I thought that two adventures in one week were sufficient for me. I heard later that Miss Jones thoroughly enjoyed the joke herself and fully admitted the efficacy of the remedy.

At that time there were many homes about the country for such cases as the two ladies whom I have just mentioned. They still flourish, so apparently people still behave in such a strange fashion in spite of the attentions of the modern psychologist.

Shortly afterwards, I said good-bye to my friends in Parkstone and Bournemouth and went to Dublin to take a post-graduate course in Obstetrics and Gynæcology. My criticisms of the general hospitals in Dublin apply with even greater force to these special hospitals. There are far too many of them but it is difficult to see how centralization can be effected in face of prejudice and reactionary spirit. But graduates come from all parts of the world to gain practical experience of these important subjects in Dublin and they are to be found to-day occupying responsible positions in many countries. For instance, there is the suave and versatile Professor Dobbin in Cairo and Dr. Hafez Affifi Pasha, the popular Egyptian Ambassador in London, who was an eminent medical practitioner before he embarked on the rough seas of Egyptian politics.

I now started in private practice in Liverpool where I

had many ups and downs, inevitable in a city already overcrowded with doctors. But social conditions in the city were then fairly good. Wages in many branches of industry were high, unemployment was almost unknown and the pubs did a roaring trade. Many of the descendants of the ordinary folk who owned them have now become members of the aristocracy. But in the midst of all this extravagant waste and almost unbelievable squalor, there was little money for the doctor. My post-graduate course, however, came in very useful. At that time a violent controversy was raging concerning the usefulness of electricity in the treatment of tumours of the womb, a form of treatment which had been introduced by Dr. Apostoli of Paris. At medical meetings and in the journals, the discussions became more and more acrimonious, the principal protagonists being the Keiths of Edinburgh and the redoubtable Lawson Tait of Birmingham. The former declared that they were so convinced of the advantage of the new treatment that they had abandoned altogether the use of the knife. Tait went to Paris to investigate the matter on the spot, but afterwards admitted that he never saw Dr. Apostoli. I went to Paris myself one summer and remained a month with Apostoli at whose clinic I met prominent doctors from all over the world. I was so impressed by what I saw that I returned again the following year to continue my investigations. As a result, I had the requisite electrical apparatus installed in my clinic and successfully practised the treatment during my stay in Liverpool. I know many people who are enjoying good health to-day thanks to it, people who before undergoing the treatment were physical wrecks.

In those days, it savoured of quackery to employ electricity as a curative agent. Our severest critics were those completely ignorant of the fundamental laws of electricity. It is not easy in a humanitarian profession to understand the blind prejudices of such people. No one in those days, however, could foresee the vast development of electricity as a cure for so many diseases. But progress has not been made without exacting its toll. Very few of the pioneers survive. Many of them have died tragic and painful deaths. I know of only one man prominent in electrical work then who is still alive now.

I read many papers before gynæcological societies on my experiences in Paris but it was like whistling for the wind to expect these distinguished gentlemen to respond to new ideas. One might have been appealing for spiritual aid, the spirit of the breezes represented in Egypt by the power of the panting lion.

But of all the controversies of this period, none caused more excitement than the wonderful discovery of Tuberculin by Koch. All roads leading to Berlin were crowded with doctors racing at top speed to obtain the new cure. Koch said that consumption in its early stages could be cured with certainty by his remedy, and that advanced cases of the disease could be temporarily arrested. Absolutely cruel hopes were held out to the poor consumptive. Notices frequently appeared in the lay press announcing that a certain doctor had just returned from a visit to Dr. Koch, and this was sufficient in itself to attract the credulous, so quickly had the new treatment caught the fancy of the public. I remember one very prominent physician in Liverpool at the time who made

D*

the pilgrimage with the usual announcement in the press. He unfortunately had enemies who were not slow in taking advantage of his absence. He was a notorious visitor at one of the well known bars in the city and a caustic colleague was heard to make one of the few jokes of his life, suggesting that he should have a label marked with the bar's name on his back in case he got lost on his way to Berlin.

The Tuberculin Cure had especial interest for me, far more than I ever expected when I first heard of it. After a severe attack of influenza, two of the most prominent physicians in Liverpool said that I was suffering from pulmonary tuberculosis. The bacillus had not long been discovered and ordinary people went about in great terror of it. Even that pleasant indoor sport of kissing was sorely neglected for a time. Fortunately, when the scare was over, it soon regained its lost popularity. My doctor insisted on my seeing an example of the terrible agent of destruction then enjoying itself in my lungs. When the inspection was over, I cheerfully said that it would be a disgrace to my name and nationality to allow myself to be extinguished by such insignificant specimens. He was terribly shocked at my levity. I went, however, to see a great authority on the disease in London and received the same verdict, but he only gave me six months to live instead of the year which the other doctors had allowed me.

They insisted on my going to the Riviera and I had a terrible fight there, not only against the bacillus but also against the mistral, bad food, cold hotels and the nauseous odour of creosote from which it was quite impossible to escape. I felt that under such conditions, the army of germs in my body might win a victory, so when I saw an advertisement about a cruise in the Mediterranean in a beautifully fitted steam yacht, I immediately returned to London to go on board at Tilbury. As we steamed down the Thames, the band—far worse than any jazz band that I have ever heard since then—struck up "Home Sweet Home". To our dismay, the tune proved to be singularly appropriate, at least in so far as our desires were concerned, for we encountered a terrific storm and lay helpless off Ushant with a big hole in the steamer's side caused by the anchor getting loose.

I returned to Liverpool from that miserable trip much worse than when I left, but with care, good food and many bottles of stout, my health was finally restored. I have had many troubles since I was sentenced to an ignominious death over forty years ago by seven doctors but even now the recollection of their grave and often sympathetic looks never fails to cheer me in the most despondent mood. At the same time, I gratefully remember the unselfish doctors who attended me at that difficult time.

I cannot say that I have the same feelings towards some other members of the profession. Some years previously, I had wanted to insure my life and was sent to a distinguished Liverpool consultant. He told me that I had heart trouble and advised me to go to the Head Office of the Insurance Company in London. There I was examined by two elderly doctors who spent over half an hour listening to the pump performing its duty. Eventually I got impatient and told them plainly that any normal, self-respecting heart would resent such unwarrantable interference. In fairness to their memory, it must be admitted that the slightest alteration in the rhythm of the heart beat was then considered by some doctors as equivalent to the death sentence. Anyhow, they both agreed with the Liverpool doctor and recommended some preposterous addition to my premium.

Unable completely to forget my unfortunate experiences with my medical advisers in Liverpool, and having more night work than was good for the most robust person, I gave up my practice there and left for Florence. I had been told that there was an opening for an English doctor there but on arrival I found three English and two American practitioners in residence. I was naturally somewhat depressed about my prospects but my new colleagues received me so kindly that I remained.

In spite of its atrocious climate, Florence was then an ideal city in which to live. Food was cheap and good and taxes almost negligible. Most of the beautiful villas in the surrounding districts were occupied by British and Americans, mostly wealthy people who had come there to escape the heavy taxation in their own country, although they pretended that the healthy climate had attracted them.

Florence was then known as the City of *Pensions* as well as of Flowers, and all these *pensions* were full of spinster ladies whose chief occupation was gossip. There were various cliques, each attached to a church, chapel or proselytizing agency, all bent on one purpose, the saving of the souls of others, especially the benighted people among whom they considered that they lived. Apparently the first step towards their salvation was to talk as much scandal about them as possible.

It was a strange and sad fact that such a beautiful city

as Florence, full of centuries of art, harboured more meanness and narrow-mindedness than many far uglier and less cultured cities. Gossip and scandal were then tolerated with benignant neutrality when not actively supported as the spice of life.

It certainly seemed incongruous to hear a lady expounding the tenets and hallucinations of Mary Eddy in a city so intimately associated with such men as Dante, Petrarch and Leonardo da Vinci.

The Italian doctors at that time were extremely courteous and correct in their professional attitude towards their foreign colleagues. There were very few restrictions for the foreign practitioners. The laws have been made more strict now but British doctors can still practise in Italy by simply having their diplomas registered. There is a reciprocal treaty between the two countries. But Italy is finished for foreign doctors now; the Italians nearly all speak English, their fees are low and many of them have married British or American women. In addition, taxation has increased to such an extent that a former colleague of mine in Florence recently told me that he had retired because he was taxed far more than he made in fees.

There was another difficulty with which we had to contend. Many British people openly assert that they prefer foreign doctors to their own men, and their numbers are increasing. There are no geographical limits to this unpardonable and unjustifiable slight to British medicine. I have heard it in Egypt, in Italy and even in England and from people who pose as Imperialists. This lack of confidence in one's own national doctors does not exist in other countries. And yet in Italy, for instance, the medical treatment of the sick is considerably hampered by the lack of skilled nursing. For some unaccountable reason, girls of the educated classes refuse to join the nursing profession, considering it undignified and unsuitable for their position in the social scale. This seems all the more strange considering the innumerable institutions that reveal the benevolence of the Italian character in an active manner. Several of them are of very ancient date. The Confraternita della Misericordia has been in existence for more than five hundred years and is entirely devoted to the care of the sick.

During my time in Florence, I frequently went in the summer to Rencegno in the Trentino as the guest of my friend, Dr. Weizz, the proprietor of the Spa and the Grand Hotel. The Trentino then belonged to Austria but the peasants (who nearly all suffered from goitre) spoke Italian and were Italian in their sympathies. The waters were very strong in arsenic. It was one of the few spas that I have ever visited where that elusive agent, radio-activity, has not been loudly proclaimed. The Rencegno arsenical waters certainly possessed remarkable virtues as a tonic and general restorative. I was so impressed by their effect and the cures which they achieved that Dr. Weizz asked me to represent the Spa at the International Medical Congress at Budapest in 1909 and read a paper on my experiences.

None could equal, however, the experience of the Congress itself. I have never seen such a collection of wild-looking men, more like bandits from the mountains than doctors. I could hardly believe that they were members of the medical profession. They came mostly from the Balkans, Ukraine, Transylvania, Rumania and

Poland. The various scientific lectures were poorly attended but when refreshments were served, there was a wild rush and almost free fights took place. Doctors and their wives and children fell over one another in their hurry to grab some food. When gorged to satiety, they seized everything within reach and stuffed it into bags especially brought for the purpose. The primitive instinct of fighting for food still seems very strong among Slav medical men. If they struggle for patients with the same ferocity as food, the unfortunate sick people must have a rough time.

One evening at the Hungaria Hotel, we were discussing the wild scenes which we had witnessed during the day and the possibility of any of the fierce men finding their way to a reception which the Archduke was giving that night for the representatives of various governments. A bet was made that none of our party would attend the function. In spite of the advice of my friends, I took up the challenge and shortly afterwards departed for the Royal Palace. I had no difficulty whatsoever in gaining admission. The scene inside was magnificent with most of the men in dazzling court dress and the women glittering with jewels. But all the same it was somewhat dull for anyone alone, so I soon took my departure. I noticed, however, that the buffet was well patronized here also but with a shade more decorum than at the conference.

The Archduke Francis-Ferdinand seemed to me a man of very strong character. He looked reticent, undemonstrative and alert with decision marked in his every movement. It was probably owing to his resolute and dominating character that he met such a tragic fate a few years later at Serajevo. Before leaving, I introduced myself to Dr. Pavy, the celebrated physician, who officially represented the British Government.

One of my most pleasant recollections of my time in Florence is my friendship with the novelist, William Le Queux. He was a strange man and obviously liked to surround himself with an atmosphere of mystery. I often doubted whether there was very much behind his innumerable impenetrable secrets; but he certainly had a very intimate knowledge of the secret services of many countries, especially Germany and Russia, and some of his novels were based on personal experiences. Le Queux was a friend of the late Lord Northcliffe and it was on his advice that he wrote his famous book on an imaginary invasion of the East Coast of England. At the time many people considered the idea completely fantastic but it was not many years before it became a grim reality. When I knew him, Le Queux was some sort of a diplomatic representative of the Republic of San Marino. I accompanied him one day when he paid one of his official visits. We motored to Bologna where we stayed the night. The next morning he appeared in the most wonderful official uniform that I have ever seen, even including the extraordinary ones of some of the officials in Cairo. It was plastered with gold lace and braid. When we arrived at the town of San Marino on the crest of a rocky mountain over two thousand feet high, we were received by the Council of Twelve and the Army chiefs. As private physician to the Consul, I shared in the honours and also attended the banquet in the evening at which Le Queux made a rousing speech in Italian. Years afterwards when I saw that San Marino had de-

clared war on the central powers, I felt that Germany's
fate was sealed. The independence of this little republic,
the last of the Italian republics, has repeatedly been
threatened, even by Napoleon, but it has always been
saved by the magnificent efforts of the inhabitants.

I had another interesting experience in connection
with a famous author at that time. Mark Twain was then
living in a furnished villa near Florence, and a dinner was
given in his honour by the British and American residents. I was asked to propose the health of the famous
humorist, perhaps the greatest of his day, and after
refusing the honour twice I finally rose with but a faint
idea of what I was going to say. I was told afterwards
that I acquitted myself satisfactorily, a remarkable
achievement considering that there was little to stimulate
me in the meal of macaroni, tough birds and sour chianti.

I remember, that I made good use of a story which I
had just heard concerning the guest of the evening. At
that period innumerable bougies were to be found in
hotel bedrooms abroad, and guests were charged one
shilling apiece for them whether they used them or not.
Even if the wick was only lighted for a moment, there
was no escaping payment and the hotel servants were
often said to light them so as to increase the guest's bill.
The story ran that Mark Twain, on leaving one of these
hotels, told the crowd outside that the Manager had
charged him a shilling each for bougies which he had
never used. Then he took a number of bougies out of his
pocket, gave them to the crowd and advised them to sell
them to the management. On entering his cab, he saw a
man standing near and gazing expectantly at him. The
great humorist asked him whether he had done anything

for him, and the latter replied that he was just watching him get into his cab, on which he immediately received a bougie as a reward.

After spending some time in Florence, I made an important decision which was to affect my subsequent career far more than I imagined at the time. The Land of the Pharoahs then appeared to be the happy hunting ground of the rich and I made up my mind to try my luck there as a doctor, thinking that it should offer a good field for medical operations. I was not mistaken.

In those days, Egypt was a very different country for visitors from what it is to-day. Wealthy British and American families used to come for long periods during the winter months. There were no empty hotels from Cairo to Assuan, and even the hotels at Heliopolis and Heluan were well patronized. Now Heluan is in a barren wilderness and the famous hotel there was converted into a sanatorium for consumptive patients many years ago. Yet before then it was crowded with travellers from all parts of the world.

There has certainly been a dramatic change. Egypt is no longer one of the world's most fashionable tourist centres. Its decay in this respect has been brought about by various things. In the first place, the amalgamation of the big hotels has been a great mistake. At one time there were two different companies competing with each other, and as a result of this healthy competition, prices were reasonable and the service was good. When the amalgamation was taking place, it was said that prices would be lowered still more but once the monopoly was firmly in the saddle, quite the reverse has been the case. The tourist industry was one of the chief sources of revenue in Egypt. Everyone benefited from it, from the railways and the vendors of spurious antiques to the donkey boys. It is one of the many mysteries of Egyptian politics why the government allowed such an amalgamation to take place when it was obviously injurious to the best interests of the country.

The invasion of a certain class of tourist, arriving in transatlantic liners during the height of the season, frequently gave rise to scenes reminiscent of Margate front on a Bank Holiday, especially if two or three steamers arrived at Alexandria on the same day. The regular visitors were swamped and becoming discontented left in large numbers, vowing never to return. Then the American slump occurred and the invasion gradually ceased. Soon we were once more dependent on the regular type of visitor and tourist only to find that he had almost completely disappeared.

Now that the Egyptians have complete control of their domestic affairs, anything may happen. Perhaps the unfortunate tourist will be treated with more consideration in every respect and the country will once again become a paradise for the travelling public, notwithstanding the changed climatic conditions. But many improvements will have to be made. Street pests of the vilest description have become such an annoyance to visitors that I used to advise my patients to wear a tarboosh and to learn a few simple yet significant Arab expressions in order to escape from their attentions.

Under the altered conditions, with no British police, it must be confessed that the outlook is gloomy. When I first arrived in Egypt, there were two more hotels than there are to-day, the Savoy and the Ghezirah Palace.

The closing of the latter was a great loss to me. The drains were supposed to be faulty, always a reliable source of income for a doctor. Typhoid fever was much more prevalent a quarter of a century ago than it is to-day. It was also much more serious in character. This is said to be the result of prophylactic vaccination but it is nothing of the sort. Improved hygienic conditions have been the main agent in bringing about this happy state of affairs. Typhoid, like typhus, is dying a natural death.

But up till 1914, Egypt was an El Dorado for the medical profession. Besides the rich tourists who came to gratify their tastes for amusement and pleasure, there were many convalescents and invalids who came to recuperate on the banks of the Nile on the advice of their doctors. Egypt was then the fashion, largely made so by the fashionable doctors who can undoubtedly make or mar health resorts. Large numbers who came to Egypt in search of health should never have been sent there; the climate was completely unsuited to them but they only discovered this when it was too late. It was the doctors sending them who were to blame. They should have known better, and in many cases I venture to think that they probably did. But Egypt was the fashion and that solved many problems.

In 1913 I was appointed English physician to the well-known Hungarian Spa of Bad Postyen. The Hungarian Government allowed me to practise there in the summer months and gave me a handsome monthly salary, while I returned to Cairo for the winter season.

The arrangement worked very well to the advantage of both the Spa and myself, for in the spring of 1914 I introduced fourteen patients from Cairo alone. Many others arrived from England and America to undergo the cure which was a most remarkable one.

It consisted of using "volcanic mud from the bowels of the earth"—so ran its advertisement—for a variety of ailments. When I first visited the place, knowing that mud was artificially heated at other health centres, I asked the director if the cure was genuine. He asked me if I could swim and when I replied that I could, we proceeded in a small boat to the middle of the river. There we plunged into the water. I found that it was very warm and on nearing the banks that the mud at the bottom was quite hot besides being unusual in colour and consistency. I soon came to the conclusion that the mud used in the cure was a natural product, volcanic in origin, and later was completely satisfied that it undeniably relieved arthritis and other rheumatic conditions.

It was certainly a very interesting if not mysterious place, but then mystery has always been associated to some extent with such health giving places ever since Thoth reigned as the Egyptian god of medicine, and was depicted as a cynocephalus ape which was greatly revered throughout the country from the most ancient times.

The mud from Bad Postyen was exported to foreign countries including America and was used with great success by many doctors in the relief of human suffering, but how it acted was a complete mystery. Among the many theories put forward by various scientists, the idea that its powers were due to radio activity naturally played a large part, for almost every medical achievement is now said to be the result of that elusive agent.

It is a curious fact about this volcanic mud and the

mud heated artificially in the local mineral waters at other Spas that once radio activity is advertised, success is assured. It is the same with many of the famous mineral waters on the Continent. The magic words of radio activity work wonders with a gullible public who seem to invite the imposition by their very stupidity. The mere mention of radio activity is sufficient in many cases to make the sufferers feel better. The influence of the mind (so easily impressed) over diseased matter makes one think of the subjective powers exercised by magicians in ancient times. The modern charlatan is no less skilful in their use. The ancient magician employed incantations, so does the modern. He only has to tell the patient that the water which he advises him to drink is the strongest in radio activity in the world and that it must be consumed while walking in five minutes or it will escape into the air, and most satisfactory results are achieved.

But my work in this delightful place was brought to an abrupt end by the outbreak of war. I shall never forget the fateful Sunday afternoon when the news of the Serajevo tragedy reached some of us as we were having tea in a café. It was a bombshell for everyone. I was absolutely convinced that we were on the brink of a terrible catastrophe. The sight of the grief-stricken head nurse of the Archduke's orphaned children, who was then staying at the Thermia Palace Hotel, only increased the tension and the gloom that settled over everything.

I have heard it said that the Archduke was unpopular. He may have been among the pleasure seeking and irresponsible Habsbourgs in Vienna, but in Hungary I cannot believe that such poignant grief was not genuine.

The Requiem in the spacious Parish Church was most impressive. Its solemnity was intensified by the deep tragic silence observed by the large congregation before, during and after the service. The whole population seemed moved to the very depths.

My gloomy presentiments cannot entirely be attributed to the murder of the Archduke. Various incidents which I witnessed among the many Germans at the Spa added to my uneasiness. Their main subject of conversation at night over their wine was the coming war. I became interested and joined them at their tables which I could easily do owing to my position as one of the Spa doctors. I was amazed at the complete lack of restraint in their conversation and the utterly stupid and boastful way in which they spoke of their plans for the conquest of half the countries in Europe.

I listened with amazement to a new map of the world being sketched out before me. Canada, of course, was to be annexed to Germany and even the Channel Islands were to become a German base. Years after the war I met one of these bombastic Germans in Cairo and took the opportunity of reminding him of his previous remarks. He actually denied everything and was most indignant when I suggested that he had a most convenient memory.

Throughout all July 1914, it was obvious to everyone in the Spa that something serious was brewing. People were to be seen everywhere talking in undertones and behaving in a very subdued manner. The Germans suddenly and mysteriously disappeared. I realized, however, that the people in England were still comparatively unaware of the seriousness of the situation when on July 15th I received a letter from Sir Bertram Dawson, now

Viscount Dawson, saying that he was sending me three lady patients for the cure. I naturally never heard any more about them.

Towards the end of July, general mobilization was ordered and the whole place was completely transformed in a day. On August 1st, the hotels were deserted and no one could be found to take our luggage to the station. It was eventually accomplished with the assistance of a huge Hungarian gypsy from the neighbouring mud village who had never done any manual labour of any sort before in his life.

The scenes at the station and the small ones through which we passed were heart-rending. Grief-stricken old men and women and young children were standing in groups, all wailing and giving vent to loud lamentations. These poor people obviously felt that they were saying good-bye to their boys for ever and in many cases it was only too true.

All this weeping and wailing presented a very sad spectacle, intensified by the utter confusion that prevailed everywhere and the drunkenness of some of the newly mobilized troops.

After eight hours' travelling we arrived at Presbourgh, now Bratislave, normally a two hours' journey. There was barely standing room in a carriage packed with drunken soldiers. Through the good offices of a Hungarian officer who was a friend of mine, we secured accommodation for the night in the town which was swarming with troops. On the following morning we left in the electric train for Vienna. We were objects of friendly attention from our fellow passengers who were extremely anxious to know the probable attitude of

England in the coming struggle. I assured them that England would be neutral although I knew it to be false. I was accompanied by a Canadian who had come for the cure and I introduced him as a retired general to gain some military support for my opinion. He enthusiastically backed me up. A more unmilitary figure it would be hard to find and it was a serious blunder to make such an assertion in a time of such excitement and extreme tension, but fortunately suspicion and hatred had not yet entered into men's mind. During the entire journey I was on tenterhooks, never knowing what would happen from one minute to another. My companion had a habit of beginning every sentence with the words "suppose" or "supposing" and he indulged in it to such an extent that I had to tell him over and over again it was a time for action, quick and decisive, and not for supposition. It had little effect, however, and he talked incessantly, always supposing this and supposing that in a most unmilitary fashion.

At last I realized that the situation was becoming rather unpleasant and that something must be done before any serious harm was done by my garrulous companion. Now he was obsessed as a patient by the then fashionable condition known as auto-intoxication. Previously it had been his sole topic of conversation but he had obviously been too frightened by the general state of affairs to mention it on this journey. I could not drop him a hint to be careful as all the passengers were too interested in him and his conversation, so seizing a favourable opportunity I said that I hoped there had been no fresh developments in his auto-intoxication as a result of all we had gone through. The trap succeeded admirably. I had to listen to a bewildering list of symptoms such as only auto-intoxication can produce.

When we said good-bye to our fellow passengers on reaching Vienna, only one thought was in my mind—the cruelty, the inhumanity and the savagery of war. Here we were in the midst of a noble and friendly race, receiving nothing but civility from them, and yet in less than a week many of them were probably blown to pieces by our countrymen on the Western front, or by the murderous Serbs in the South.

A dark ominous cloud seemed to be hanging over Vienna which presented a most dismal appearance. There was no evidence of any enthusiasm anywhere, apart from the miserable attempts of some youngsters at demonstrations. There was a constant stream of officers' motor cars towards the War Office, but nothing else to indicate that anything serious had happened, although at that time war had been declared against Serbia.

With the greatest difficulty I managed to get on board a military train for Trieste, having seen my fictitious general off to Paris a few hours previously. Just as his train was about to start he said: "Now suppose this train is stopped at the frontier . . ." But fortunately the whistle then blew and I did not hear the rest of his gloomy forebodings.

My companions in the railway carriage to Trieste were all officers on their way to the Serbian front. The same lack of enthusiasm was noticeable there as in the capital. One of the officers, a married man with children, told me that he was employed in a large shop in Vienna and that war was far from being his profession. In fact, he obviously detested the whole business. I often wondered how many of these peaceful, sober, industrious men returned to their homes and families, and how many of them were buried in the hated soil of the semi-civilized barbarians whom they were on their way to fight. The Serbs are and always have been disturbing elements in international politics. I think that they will be the source of serious trouble again in the future. The country is seething with discontent which is kept at boiling point by secret societies in some of which black-magic is said to play a sinister part.

On arrival in Trieste I immediately went to the British Consul for advice. He was brief and to the point: "Get out of here as quickly as you can, I am leaving in an hour." There was an air of gloom without the slightest sign of enthusiasm in Trieste also. Numerous regiments were to be seen, all proceeding in the same direction and obviously Slav from their hang-dog looks. I never saw a regimental band accompanying any of them. I was not at all surprised to hear later of the treachery and cowardice of Czech and Slav regiments in face of the enemy.

While at Trieste I could not help recalling a very disagreeable incident of the previous year. In pre-war days, the cabmen, police and other officials were notorious for their rudeness to foreigners, and the cabmen for their extortionate charges. On my arrival from Vienna, a cabman drove me to the steamer. He demanded an exorbitant fare and I refused to pay it. There was the inevitable scene. Sometime afterwards I went ashore and the cabman rushed after me and told a pack of lies to a policeman with an enormous sword who insisted on taking me to the police station. I was in a frightful rage, shook my fist in his face several times and told him that if I had a sword half as long as his, there would be trouble. On my release, I went straight to the British Consulate. A dago was in charge and he tried to ignore my protest but I insisted on his sending for the Commandant of the Police. I refused to be satisfied until the latter sent for the policeman who had arrested me. I took his number and said that the matter would be reported to the British Ambassador at Vienna, but on the Commandant promising to take disciplinary measures I agreed to do nothing.

It was with the greatest difficulty that I succeeded in getting a train to Italy and eventually to Brindisi. It was now August 3rd. It was a scorching day and I had a terrible journey. The Italians were very excited and positively rude to some poor Austrian subjects on their way to Egypt. It looked at one time as if hostilities would break out before the declaration of war. It must be remembered that at this time Italy was in alliance with the central powers. On arrival at Brindisi which is always a miserable hole, I found that my real troubles were only just beginning. The place was crowded with refugees of all nationalities. No accommodation was to be had except loathsome lodgings full of bugs and insects. In addition, I was penniless. My Austrian money was worthless and the very possession of it aroused unpleasant suspicions. I had to spend ten days in this miserable plight. If it had not been for the British Vice-Consul, an Irishman named Sinclair, I do not know what I should have done. I visited him every day and he always cheered me up with a drink and finally paid my passage to Egypt. Through his good offices, I obtained permission to travel on a small steamer having accommodation for thirty passengers. When I arrived, I found that there were already three hundred and fifty passengers on board, nearly all sleeping on deck packed like sardines. I found an unoccupied spot under the bridge and settled down with a bottle of whisky as companion which the good Consul had packed unbeknown to me with some other things. Unfortunately some of my fellow passengers discovered the nature of my luggage, judging from the numbers who came to visit me. It eventually dawned upon me that it was "leetle wheskee" that they wanted. We had an uneventful voyage thanks to fine weather. There was nothing to break the monotony except the sight of innumerable French war craft. The only other excitement was the difficulty of getting anything to eat, even a hard crust of bread, or a little water in which to wash one's hands; to drink it, of course, would have been to court disaster.

I reached Cairo at last, twenty-two days after leaving Hungary.

I might mention here that when I wished to return to Bad Postyen and resume my former position after the war, I was horrified to discover that the territory had been forcibly taken away from the noble Hungarians and handed over to the treacherous Czechs by the infamous Treaty of Trianon. In spite of the active intervention of the British Minister and Consul at Prague and the demands of the Directors of the Spa, the Czech Government refused to allow me to return to practice there. Knowing them as I do, I was not at all surprised, especially as I learned afterwards that many Austrian and Hungarian doctors were treated in exactly the same way. They had spent all their lives in the country and in their case it amounted to sheer brutality. The slogan of the

Czechs was, and is, Czecho-Slovakia for the Czechs. This exaggerated form of nationalism is hardly in the best interests of the country. It has created insurmountable obstacles to true national growth and considerably hampers the fusion of widely different races on a basis of real equality and fraternity.

They even went so far as to alter the names of places to make them conform to their own brand of nationalism. The old established Spa of Carlsbad is now called Karlovy Vary, and of course Bad Postyen sounded too Teutonic for the patriotic Czechs and its name has now been changed at my suggestion, to Pistany, a shortened form of the Slav Piestany. When local nationalism descends to such trivialities, one is almost inclined to wish for another Teutonic invasion to bring the inhabitants to their senses.

N.B. Since writing the above, my predictions have been fulfilled.

IV

SHORTLY after my arrival in Cairo, I received a local commission as Captain. To obtain a regular commission, it was necessary to report to the War Office in London and then probably to be sent back to Egypt again. This was a typical example of the methods of the military authorities in Whitehall. It is surprising that such stringent red-tape allowed them to muddle through anything.

I was appointed to the Fever and Dysentry Wards of the Citadel Hospital. I doubt whether a more unsuitable building for a hospital could have been found in the whole of Egypt, and yet it is still used for the same purpose to-day. At that time it was alive with bugs. I used to see them fall from the rotten old wooden ceilings on to the beds of the poor Tommies too weak to knock them on to the floor without the assistance of a nurse. Such horrible sights were a common occurrence, but it was not the fault of the hospital staff. In spite of all our efforts, it was quite impossible to get rid of them. We tried everything. As soon as a bed became vacant—and many vacancies occurred daily—the whole framework was treated with an alcoholic flame. The bedding was also thoroughly disinfected but nothing seemed to have any appreciable effect on the invasion. The incoming soldiers were doubtless accompanied by their inseparable comrades who remained with them in spite of all the precautions that were taken to destroy them. As for the rats, they behaved as if the whole place belonged to them. They actually bit some of the V.A.D.'s.

And yet in that unhygienic building, there were several thousand patients packed so closely together that there was scarcely room for the big rats to play. Most of the patients came from Gallipoli and Palestine. Many were in a terrible condition and so emaciated that they looked more like mummies than human beings. It was quite common to find a soldier suffering from enteric, malaria and dysentery all at the same time. Many cases had been wrongly diagnosed as dysentery and the treatment had invariably been the same. Chlorodyne had always been administered and nothing could have been worse. The result was that nearly all the poor fellows were dangerously toxic on arrival. Although it seemed almost hopeless to try to save their lives, the small percentage of deaths was truly remarkable. This was largely due to good nursing and a suitable diet.

The hospital staff were the most motley crowd that I have ever met. Every imaginable kind of doctor seemed to have been recruited for the service. It was a most strange atmosphere. At times in the mess, when the main topics of conversation were salaries and the previous night's adventures, it was difficult to realize that all these men were there to fight for the lives of their fellows in the midst of one of the greatest tragedies that the world has ever seen. But the grim situation with all its sadness, incredible suffering and all prevalent death had its humorous side. The interminable discussions about the extra allowances were almost unbelievable. If it so happened that sixpence a day was deducted, a deputation immediately interviewed the unfortunate head of the hospital. I soon discovered that it is a mistake to believe in conscientious work in the army. It is obviously even more reprehensible to express open dislike of extravagance, duplicity and meanness, for it is fatal to one's own peace of mind, advancement and popularity. I never knew until then that such jealousy, back-biting and calumny could enter into the fibre of so-called educated men. In time of war, among men who should have been united in their efforts to relieve suffering, there seemed even less excuse for it.

In spite of all these difficulties, however, I enjoyed my work at the Citadel Hospital. For one thing, I was extremely gratified at the result of my own work. I had no deaths in the typhoid group of patients and only about one per cent among the dysenteries.

In addition to my exacting hospital duties, I acted as Honorary Secretary to the St. John Ambulance Association at the request of Colonel Rawnsley. When the Association was amalgamated with the Red Cross, I served on the executive committee for the duration of the war. I often examined and lectured to the innumerable V.A.D.'s of all nationalities who served in the local hospitals. On one occasion I asked a doctor from some place in Asia Minor to lecture to a number of girls who had come from the same district. He was supplied with diagrams and the usual regulation text books but when I came to examine them, I found that they were all completely ignorant even of the most elementary details of the subject. It was an awkward predicament, but as they were destined to work only among their own national refugees, they were passed *en bloc*. I afterwards heard that they did excellent work among the destitute people in the concentration camps. There are some occasions when practice is obviously worth more than years of theoretical study.

In spite of some bickering about minor matters, the executive committee did excellent work. The equipment of the well appointed hospital at Giza was ample proof of this. We were honoured by a visit from His Royal Highness the Duke of Connaught during the war and the members of the Committee were presented to him. In the evening I was invited to dinner at the Residency to meet His Royal Highness who took me aside afterwards and questioned me minutely about my Red Cross work, giving me the impression that he was greatly interested. I much appreciated the compliment considering all the difficulties which I encountered in less exalted spheres at the time.

After several months at the Citadel Hospital, General Ford, D.M.S. sent for me and deliberately launched me on a sea of troubles, asking me to take charge of the European Lock Hospital where the conditions were said to be simply appalling.

I inspected the hospital and then went straight to the D.M.S. and told him that I was absolutely horrified by what I had seen, adding that even at the risk of insubordination I could not possibly be associated with a hospital in such a condition and that it was a positive disgrace to all concerned.

He showed me particulars concerning the ravages of disease among the troops and some reports concerning gross irregularities in connection with the hospital but I remained adamant.

The following day General Maxwell sent for me and repeating what the D.M.S. had said, earnestly appealed to me to take over the management of the hospital for a short time until radical improvements could be made. From an hygienic point of view, the situation was very serious and even alarming. Months after decisive action should have been taken, the authorities were beginning to realize that something would have to be done about it. I found myself faced with a very difficult problem. On the one hand, personal considerations made me aware that acceptance of the post would mean embarking on a sea of troubles and that I would do well to decline any share of responsibility in the solution of a thankless and unsavoury problem; on the other, a sense of public duty and the desire to relieve suffering urged me to accept the difficult task. Against the advice of my friends, I finally accepted the position but only on the understanding that all defects would be remedied.

It is quite impossible for me to describe now what I saw when I first inspected the hospital. The sanitary, hygienic, medical and administrative arrangements could only adequately be mentioned in a medical journal; they would make too unpleasant reading for the general reader. But here are a few details which I consider fit for publication.

The internal conditions were as bad as they could possibly be. There was only one sterilizer and I was told that it was never used. Instruments used in highly infective cases were simply dipped into a weak solution of Lysol. No attempt at sterilization by boiling was ever made.

The women were all crowded into one small room for

examination, possibly to allow them to escape from the squalid waiting-room which contained nothing but dirty wooden benches. The walls were bare and there was not a single peg on which they could hang their hats or clothes. They had to put them on the floor or dirty benches.

Fleas, lice, mosquitoes, flies and bed bugs abounded. The unfortunate patients complained bitterly about them, but what they complained most about was the rats which disported themselves freely and openly everywhere. Although the hospital had been open for several months, I could find no trace whatsoever of any clinical record of the cases admitted. There were a few bed sheets but no record of any bacteriological tests, and there was no proper record of the treatment employed except in a few cases. No supervision seemed to have been exercised over the native nurses, whose training had simply consisted of three months in a general hospital for natives. Under such circumstances it was not surprising that there was a grave suspicion of the propagation of disease. The conditions were certainly more conducive to the spreading of disease than to its cure.

Some half-hearted attempts had been made to rectify these disgraceful conditions but nothing had really been done. At this time every soldier was needed at the front and every effort should have been made to render as many men as possible fit for active service, but officialdom was otherwise engaged. Incompetence and arrogance with the addition of vanity as a comic element and innumerable quarrels about insignificant trifles for a long time formed an effective barrier against any progress. Everyone was agreed that certain alterations and improvements were essential but it nevertheless took several months, with much opposition from various departments, before anything was done. It was not really until the whole matter had been thoroughly investigated by a Military Court of Inquiry that any radical improvements were made. It sat for three weeks and nearly a hundred witnesses were examined and as a result of all this waste of time and money, those responsible for the mal-administration of the hospital were severely censured while the medical officers who had been trying to contend with these appalling conditions were highly praised. But even then troubles were not at an end. Another site was chosen for the hospital but the new premises were quite unsuitable and much money was spent in trying to modernize a dilapidated building, but it was a distinct improvement on the old one. For the first time the patients were housed as human beings instead of as friendless outcasts and criminals.

This leads me to make a brief survey of one aspect of the health of the troops during the war which has not received the attention it deserves, in fact I am tempted to say that a conspiracy of silence has drawn a veil over the whole question. Hundreds of thousands of young healthy soldiers were pouring into Egypt from all parts of the Empire, into a country notorious for the prevalence of venereal disease of an especially virulent type. Nothing whatsoever was done in the early stages of the war to protect these troops with the result that they succumbed in battalions. The conditions, particularly among the Australians, assumed a very alarming aspect. To make matters worse, for some extraordinary reason they were deprived of any proper treatment in the early days, in fact they received little or no treatment of any sort. Rumours of a very disconcerting character were rife in Cairo at the time and to satisfy myself about their truth I decided to visit the military camp near the Pyramids. I have never seen such ghastly sights in all my medical experience. The camp was strongly reminiscent of the Middle Ages when sufferers from such diseases—still burdened with the stigma of Moses when he termed them unclean—were cast out and left in the fields to die. What I saw in that camp was simply a repetition of such atrocities. Hundreds of these men were sent back to Australia and Malta, ruined in health and a disgrace to themselves, their relations and their country, simply because two or three competent doctors had not been appointed to look after them.

That loathsome camp at Mena will remain an indelible disgrace to the authorities in the early history of the war in Egypt. Is it to be wondered at that the Australian soldiers made a serious attempt to burn a certain district in Cairo, including women and furniture in the holocaust? The attempt would have succeeded but for the interference of British troops.

The following extracts from an article by Sir James Barrett of Melbourne in the *British Medical Journal* in 1919 will give an idea of the conditions then prevailing among the Australian troops. He refers, however, to known cases and there were thousands treated privately by quacks, qualified and unqualified. The scandal of these charlatans became so serious that on my suggestion the military authorities forbade foreign doctors of a certain type to advertise on their plates that they were specialists in venereal diseases. They were in the habit of telling the poor soldiers that they were infected when they were not and used to demand a big fee to effect a "cure".

Sir James Barrett said: "On arrival in Egypt in January 1915 I found the military authorities were much perturbed by the amount of venereal diseases amongst the troops. Before they left for the Dardanelles, eight hundred to one thousand men were known to be suffering from venereal diseases at any one time, from two and a half to three per cent. The average stay in hospital was sixteen days, so the number of infections was large.

"In addition, 1,344 men were sent back to Australia and 450 to Malta. The cost of sending a soldier to Egypt and back to Australia with his equipment and pay has been estimated at £300. If so, the cost of these cases to the State must have been somewhere about £500,000 without any commensurate return. The number of infected was so large and the damage so great that renewed efforts were made. From January to May 1916, that is five months, there were no fewer than 10,000 known cases in Egypt. The matter was regarded as so serious that a combined civilian and military committee was appointed to investigate and recommend."

When he arrived in Egypt in January 1915, Sir James Barrett was asked by General Sir William Birdwood to start a "moral and military campaign" among the Australian troops. Incredible as it may seem, he would not authorize the use of prophylactics. Had he done so, thousands of men would unquestionably been spared for the front where they were badly needed. The Cairo Purification Committee was one of the biggest jokes of the war, both on account of its composition and the idiosyncrasies of some of the witnesses, but principally because of one of its weighty recommendations: the abolition of the Danse du Ventre in public places. Just imagine! A purification committee sitting in Cairo in the midst of a world war! Well, it afforded great amusement and that was something after all at a time of great anxiety and stress.

During all this time from 1914 to 1916, the National Council for combating venereal disease in England was doing nothing but talk. They only suggested lectures and instruction for the soldiers with proper provision for recreation. Meanwhile about a hundred loose women were pouring into Salisbury each week-end without any restriction whatsoever. It seems incredible but it is none the less true.

In later years, the worthy Chairman of the National Council, after dwelling on the grave anxiety and trouble which the large Canadian camp of over 50,000 soldiers had caused him and his colleagues, announced with becoming gravity that at last they were determined to wrestle with the evil and that a new era was opening. The Mayor and the Council had decided to appoint two women police—two policewomen to protect the morals of an army of such great numbers! They were supposed to bring about this moral revolution by trying to exercise a good influence over the thousands of harpies that preyed upon them.

It was nearly three years before the Council recommended their lecturers to advise early preventive treatment, so heavily did the hand of Mrs. Grundy press upon them. Their behaviour reminds me of the story of a Scottish missionary. At the beginning of the last century the General Assembly in Edinburgh heard very bad accounts of the drunkenness in the Highlands, so they decided to send a missionary to the North to preach temperance. On his return, the missionary appeared before the Assembly and said: "I have had gran' success." "What do you mean by 'gran' success'?" asked the Moderator. "Well," replied the missionary, "ye must know that I found the situation simply awfu' but I wrestled with the puir misguidit folk and as a result of me meenestrations they have sworn to ameliorate their habits and no take mair than a dram of whisky before breakfast the morn."

A time arrived, however, when it was forcibly brought home to all concerned that radical measures must be adopted and a campaign to put a stop to these scandals was started by the Director General with the following results.

During the month of September 1916 from among 42,000 Canadian troops in Great Britain, 960 cases suffering from venereal diseases were admitted to hospital; during the month of September 1918, from among 110,000 Canadians in Great Britain, there were only 750 such cases.

Could there be any more deadly condemnation of the ostrich like policy pursued at the beginning?

Before leaving this important subject which many of my readers are doubtless only too anxious to avoid, let us look back into the past and think of the origin and history of these mysterious maladies, which until to-day have not been very well understood and, it may be added, are not altogether satisfactorily treated even now.

The origin of venereal diseases seems to be lost in antiquity, but its very antiquity, based on Biblical references and old medical reports, has been questioned by many modern authorities. The same applies to reputed bone diseases in mummies. There is no reliable evidence to prove the existence of the disease among the Ancient Egyptians. We are almost forced to the conclusion that, like many other things, good and bad, the disease is of American origin. The Spanish sailors who accompanied Columbus were infected in Hayti in 1493, and on their arrival in Barcelona spread the disease, an easy matter considering the rapturous welcome that awaited them. Many of these sailors joined the army of Charles VIII. The soldiers now infected Naples and in a few years Europe was aflame and the fires have been raging ever since. At first it was called the Neopolitan disease or Morbus Gallicus, but in 1530 Facastorius in a classic poem called "syphilis sive Morbus Gallicus" gave it the name by which it has since been known. On the other hand, contagious diseases of the kind are believed to have existed in the early ages. For instance, they are believed to have been very prevalent among the ancient Jews and it is suggested that circumcision was invented as a possible preventive. Moses attempted to eradicate prostitution but failed; nevertheless, the hygienic and police regulations invented by him for the prevention and cure of these affections might be copied with advantage to-day. It must therefore be presumed that the wise old legislator was conversant with the dire consequences of these maladies. He doubtless had many opportunities of observing them at close quarters, considering the unhygienic mode of life and the sexual incontinence of the Children of Israel as recorded in history at that time.

In the Greek and Roman age, the moral conditions were deplorable. Juvenal exclaims: "Vice has culminated." Disease was inevitably also rampant, and to make matters worse, sufferers did not receive the best available treatment, owing to the hypocritical attitude of the leaders of the healing art. The fear of contagious diseases in the early ages was very great, and Dafour asserts that it was the dread of contracting them that accounted for the sexual perversions of the Ancient Greeks. In the Middle Ages, we find the same superstitious fear and pharisaical notions in existence. Sangers tells us that infected people were driven into the fields to die, the physicians refusing to attend the sick for fear of contracting disease. But as Thucydides rightly remarks, Prostitution has existed at all times and will always continue. But the matter has seldom been considered from the standpoint of practical policy. Special laws have certainly been made at various times in an attempt to control the evil but to no purpose. Then there have always been a class of people who objected to any official recognition of the evil on what they called moral grounds. Equally ineffective have been the Moral and Spiritual Agencies, but this is largely due to the great body of public opinion which tacitly approves the double standard of morals, and when it sees the results, murmurs meaningless platitudes about "human nature".

There is no doubt that the extremists safely ensconced behind their puritanical smoke screens, never having experienced many generous or sympathetic impulses in their lives, were directly responsible for some of the appalling conditions that prevailed among the troops during the war.

Vice is largely the reflex of social conditions, low wages and squalid homes, to which must now be added the increase in unemployment and dearer food. Apart from drastic remedial measures directed towards certain economic, social and housing conditions, reform can only be achieved by education and regulation, combined with disciplinary medical examination and treatment. Contagious diseases should be notifiable in both sexes, and blame and responsibility should be equally attached to both. It is not surprising that all the efforts made in the past to mitigate the evils of prostitution have failed when sexual irregularities are expected in men and chastity is demanded from women. The two theories are mutually destructive. Brothels should be regularly licensed and the money obtained in this way should be spent on the upkeep of special hospitals. The fact that such places were licensed would in itself be a sure guarantee that their most objectionable features, such as disorder and petty crime, ceased to exist in them. There should be specially trained doctors and the whole system controlled by a special police force of women. The ordinary police should have nothing whatsoever to do with the traffic; they are corrupt enough already in many countries.

The belief that prostitution can be eradicated is of course an Utopian dream. As already pointed out, every attempt to suppress it has ended in failure. Nearly every city has been swept at one time or another by waves of moral virtue and purity campaigns that have resulted in ill-considered crusades against the so-called social evil. For instance, in Philadelphia some years ago the better class citizens rose up against the houses of ill-fame and demanded their suppression. It was not long before a petition was laid before the City Fathers asking them to relax the severity of police control over these houses, as it had become unsafe for any respectable woman to walk in the streets unaccompanied at night. The same thing happened in Pittsburgh and recently in New York a similar effort resulted in the dissemination of vice throughout the city. More futile attempts have been made to deal with the scourge in America than in any other country, with the result that over 220,000 men are annually infected, twenty per cent of the blindness there can be attributed to the disease and there are from thirty to fifty per cent of childless marriages and eighty per cent gynæcological operations from the same cause.

I am convinced that a policy of frankness and open speaking is the only one that will improve conditions. I believe that if the medical profession in the first place, the National Council and the Government had spoken out without any reserve at the beginning of the war, the well-being and the happiness of thousands of our troops would have been preserved. Even at this late date, I would ask the National Council to influence the Government to publish a statement regarding the venereal situation in the army in successive years of the Great War, with details about the different regions—at home, in France, Mesopotamia and other places, so that the country should know how the trouble affected the army and thus gain some information with regard to its prevalence in various areas and classes of the population. I am convinced that the upholders of the bated breath and ostrich policy must realize the unreasonableness of their views in the face of certain undeniable truths. Even the politician anxious for votes need not seriously take their opposition into account now. Mrs. Grundy and the prudes are in far greater evidence in the United States than in this country, and yet the Surgeon-General of the American Army did not hesitate to publish in his routine orders in 1912 outspoken regulations, directing all soldiers returning to camp to state whether they had exposed themselves to the possibility of venereal infection, and detailing the early preventive treatment if it was necessary. If he could do so before the war in America, much could be done now in England.

There is one aspect of the situation that is not often realized; the possible repercussions of venereal diseases on the course of our contemporary history and the possibility that they may be the cause of the present troubled state of the world. Let us see what the past can teach us. There are quite a number of intelligent and honest people who believe that the greatness of England dates from the reign of Henry VIII. They may have some justification for their belief but pathological and bacteriological investigations have not yet revealed that the germ of syphilis can ever have beneficial effect on character and human actions. The whole subject demands more thorough investigation than it has yet received. But while a variety of causes undeniably contribute towards the course of human behaviour and thus towards the trend of events and history, it is equally undeniable that many infamous treaties, unjust wars (even in recent times) financial scandals and inhuman and barbaric cruelties of all kinds in all ages can be attributed to the manifestation of the greatest scourge that has ever afflicted mankind.

The tragedy of the Tudors was syphilis. The history of Henry was that of the course of his physical decay and mental deterioration as a result of this disease. He died in stupor at the age of fifty-five after a number of years of personal savagery betokening luetic mental degeneracy, during which time he suffered from obsessions, phobias and notions of divinity.

McLaurin in his remarkable book, *Mere Mortals*, assumes that he must have acquired the disease before the marriage to Katherine of Aragon at about the age of eighteen, for the long record of marital mishaps, so pathognomic of syphilis, begins with the death of Katherine's first-born son at the age of six weeks. Then came a still-birth in 1510. A son was born in 1511 who died in three days. In 1513 there was a son who was either still-born or who died immediately after birth. In 1514 another son was born who died immediately after christening. In 1516 was born Mary, whose sickliness throughout life is significant and whose portrait, revealing a wizened, lined and prematurely aged face, suggests much to the medical eye. Her sole pregnancy after her marriage to Philip of Spain is supposed to have terminated in a miscarriage. The last child of Henry and Katherine, born in 1518, was a still-born boy. To Anne Boleyn was born Elizabeth. "Whether she [Elizabeth] escaped infection is at least doubtful." Then came a miscarriage. To Jane Seymour came the frail child who as Edward VI was to die at an early age of what McLaurin believes to have been syphilis of the lung. Henry's physical degeneration was very apparent during his union with Anne Boleyn.

By the time he married Catherine Howard, his degenerated tissues were so bloated that he could hardly pass through an ordinary door. To Catherine Howard, death by beheading was preferable to life with this degenerate, and her last words on the scaffold were to that effect. It was at this time that he cleared the Tower of London by issuing orders that every prisoner in it was to be beheaded. "Thus Henry the Horrible lived in an atmosphere of disease, lust, obscenity, grandiose ideas, cowardice and loathsomeness." But for his disease, the history of England might have been very different. One wonders how far this and other organisms were responsible for the character of a certain infamous treaty and the political and economic evils that have inevitably been its result.

Medical men are hampered even now in their attempts to deal with the matter by the medieval doctrine which, though not always expressed in words, is still at work, persuading the public to regard sexual diseases from a different standpoint from that which they maintain towards all others. While the more prominent and lay promoters of the great advance in public education in these matters decline to acknowledge the importance of preventing infection at its source, it is not surprising that the medical profession as a body has not accepted full responsibility for the undertaking without more encouragement from the rest of the community.

It is undeniable that neither moral nor religious instruction will succeed in the future, any more than they have in the past, in checking the irregular gratification of the sexual instinct. The danger of venereal infection has long been held out as a deterrent, but with little or no effect. No more adequate result can be expected from the more detailed accounts of these dangers that have lately been given to the public.

Sir James Crichton-Brown once wrote as follows in a letter which he has given me full permission to use:

"If syphilis were an inevitably ordained consequence of irregular sexual intercourse, something might be said for leaving it alone; but as it is only a very occasional consequence, it ought to be prevented in every possible way.

"The prevention of syphilis and the prevention of immorality should be kept wholly distinct from each other. The Government have forbidden the sale of whisky less than three years old, the object being that in maturing it may be freed from the ingredients that produce injurious effects on the consumer. But, according to the opponents of the prevention of syphilis, that must be all wrong. The rawer the whisky, the more fusel oil in it, the better it is; so that men may be prevented from drinking by the dread of delirium tremens. I remember Lord Houghton telling me of a conversation which he had with Mrs. Butler at the time of the discussion of the Contagious Diseases Act. At last he said to her: 'It seems to me, Mrs. Butler, that you regard the syphilitic virus as a beneficial moral agent. Now tell me, if you had that virus locked up in a box, and you had the key, would you keep it locked up or would you let it loose upon humanity?'

"Mrs. Butler vouchsafed no answer. I wholly agree with the criticism in the *British Medical Journal* that effective measures of prevention must apply to both sexes.

"The dissemination of the disease by the male has

especially attracted attention of recent years owing to the large numbers of infected soldiers who returned to this country during and after the war.

"I do not hesitate to express my opinion that doctors not only are justified in spreading the knowledge we now possess of effectual prophylaxis in respect to venereal diseases, but also are bound in duty to do so in view of their knowledge of the results of the disease, and of their functions as promoters of the public health. The question is, and should be regarded as an exclusively medical one. The time has come for plain speaking and prompt action on the part of the medical profession. In the words of the article in the *Lancet*, 'preventive treatment is a logical step forward and ought to be taken at once'."

I find it difficult to understand the violent opposition, especially in Anglo-Saxon countries, to every measure calculated to minimize the results of a great evil. Can these well meaning people realize the gravity of their obstructive policy? Or is the speciousness of hypocrisy too assertive?

V

BEFORE and after the war, I took advantage of living in Cairo to learn as much as I could of Egyptian ways and customs, both ancient and modern. I found that Demonology seems to have set its stamp on Egyptian life from the very earliest times down to the present day. To the inhabitants of the Nile Valley, the spirit world has been and is very real. For them, it is peopled with demons, devils, good and evil spirits, genii, afreets, ghosts and vampires, all ready to issue forth and cause disease or misfortune to human beings. It is a curious fact that fundamentally the life of the modern Egyptian is the same as that of his ancestors thousands of years ago. I mean with regard to his religious and supernatural beliefs. Thus the present can reveal the past far more in Egypt than in many other countries where modern civilization has so completely transformed the inhabitants. By careful examination of the surviving customs and beliefs in Egypt, especially among the fellaheen of Upper Egypt and the wise old women who are to be found in the environs of Cairo, much can be learned of the life of the distant past. The excavations of the tombs may provide richly endowed universities and wealthy individuals with interesting data but in my opinion it is a sacrilegious and unprofitable practice. With a few rare exceptions, information obtained in this way has not proved to be of very serious scientific value.

The basic facts and truths of the life of the past are to be found more by a study of ancient writers, such as Herodotus, Manetho and Diodorus. The excavators have always been obliged to bolster up their inadequate knowledge obtained from the tombs themselves by continual reference to these writers.

Egypt might well be called a huge cemetery, although the inhabitants at all periods seem to have had a mortal dread of such places because of their firm belief in apparitions and ghosts, and more especially in malevolent spirits. The fear of evil spirits was so strong in ancient Egypt that it demanded costly efforts to appease them. If a place was thought to be haunted, gentle means of persuasion were first of all tried in an attempt to induce the evil spirits to leave. If these failed, threats were employed and even strong action to try to drive the spirits away by beating them out with sticks and staves.

Various devices have been employed at different times as protectors against evil influences, including iron, salt and fire. If these were successful, the ghost on departing was believed to leave a visiting card in the form of an old shoe to indicate that he had been a visitor. The reason for this strange memento remains inexplicable but possibly in this we have an explanation of the custom of throwing an old shoe after brides in modern times.

A very objectionable form of ghost of very ancient lineage is the prowling she-devil who goes about at night looking for new-born babies to devour. The Egyptian woman of to-day goes in great fear of these cannibal spirits. The usual way of dealing with them is to put a little salt and bread near the mother's pillow, like putting salt on a bird's tail when you want to catch it. Whether it is more effective or not, I cannot say.

This belief in ghosts is as general to-day as it was in ancient times and the Arabs also stand in great awe of them. The ghosts are thought to be most numerous in cemeteries, ancient tombs and the dark places of temples. They are called afreets.

A whirlwind of sand or dust is very common in Egypt and is generally believed to be due to an afreet enjoying an aerial flight. Curiously enough the same phenomenon in Ireland is usually attributed to the fairies enjoying the same thing. It is by no means uncommon to see an Irish peasant taking off his hat to them and saying, "God speed ye gintlemin". Similarly the Egyptians, on seeing a shooting star, exclaim, "May Allah transfix the enemy of the religion," believing that it is a dart thrown by God at an afreet.

It is widely believed in the villages that every person is accompanied by his carina or shadow which travels about with him from birth to death. It sometimes leaves its shadowy form and becomes a cat. The fellaheen also believes that a twin is capable at will of becoming a cat too. You therefore have to be very careful in your treatment of cats in Egypt. However hideous and maddening the nightly noises of these animals may be, you must not throw a boot at them or you may unwittingly injure the twin brother or shadow of your suffragi. In ancient Egypt, on the death of the household cat everyone went into mourning and shaved his eyebrows. And if there was a fire, it was far more important to rescue the cat than to try to put out the conflagration. With such traditions in the past, it is not surprising that the modern Egyptian treats the cat with superstitious respect.

The phenomenon of Lycanthropy or the power to transform one's self into an animal is accepted as a natural fact in many parts of Africa to-day. There are many authentic instances recorded which are not always easy to explain away. The earliest allusion comes from the war between Horus and Set and the wounding of Horus by Set in the form of a black pig. The abhorrence of swine to this day in Egypt probably proceeds from this legend, as well as the antipathy to swineherd men who are considered untouchables.

The shadow myth is by no means confined to Egypt. It is to be found in many parts of the world and is always associated with an evil influence. For instance, in Ethiopia disease is thought to be caused by the shadow of an enemy falling upon one, and among the Hawaiians people must not let their shadow fall upon the chief. In Europe I have known people to protest strongly if others walk on their shadows. Indeed in Ireland, one of my earliest recollections is the severe reprimand I received for having walked across another shadow. I was peremptorily told to recross it, presumably to nullify any possible evil effects. The ancient Egyptians thought that when the body died, the shadow departed from it and could only be brought back by the performance of a mystical ceremony in which magic played an important part.

The shadow was a very real thing among ancient peoples and there are many survivals of superstitious beliefs connected with it, such as the idea in Frazer's Island that a young woman's shadow must not pass over

the sleeping place of a young man. The expression—
"may your shadow never grow less"—which is so often
thoughtlessly used, probably has a mystical origin in the
very earliest sages.

But besides the shadow or carina, there is also the
Ukht or sister, an underground twin spirit of every
human being. The Ukht is both human and feminine in
character and like many women often causes a lot of
trouble. Not infrequently she becomes passionately
jealous of a man's human wife and contrives to kill her
children. Of course there is but one way of ending this
deadly strife and that is to visit the local wise woman and
to purchase from her a powerful charm such as a wolf's
tooth which has perhaps come from Mecca. Sometimes
it is necessary to make more than one visit, for there are
remedies for the different moods of the angry spirits.
It is extraordinary what human and realistic traits are
developed by the Ukht as skilfully analysed by these
ignorant old witches to their own profit.

These underground spirits may work good or evil and
there are innumerable charms to appease their wrath and
gain their favour. No matter what disease a person is
really suffering from, the wise woman has to be consulted. But there are many strange diseases in Egypt
including the supposed effects of Black Magic. If a
woman has worked Black Magic against another, the
latter obtains from the witch a charm which she holds
in her hand for half an hour and then keeps in her house
for several days, after which the stone is returned to the
wise woman. This is supposed to prevent her enemy's
Black Magic from taking effect. If a woman believes that
Black Magic has been used against her, she must bury

two stones, likewise obtained from the witch, under the threshold of her door and they will prevent evil spirits from entering her house. Of course the stones cost money.

The Ancient Egyptians were lavish in their expenditure on their tombs. They wanted to preserve their bodies from desecration and to provide them with all that they might require after death. The immortal part of a dead man was thought to have its special abode in the statue of the deceased. It was called the Ka, or double. A special part of the tomb was reserved for it and this was known as the Ka's House. The ancient cemeteries were looked upon as cities of living spirits. Considering that every imaginable precaution was taken for the physical and spiritual welfare of Ka, it is difficult to understand why the cemeteries where he resided inspired such terror among the inhabitants, as they still do to-day among their descendants.

When a man's ghost is giving trouble, it is exorcized by making a clay image of him. The ghost is then supposed to take up his abode in the image and to vanish as it wastes away through the influence of the elements. This may be the reason of so many statues in Egypt.

It is easy for us to laugh at some of the superstitious beliefs of the Egyptians, and yet I doubt whether we have advanced so far in our understanding of the occult to make any clear pronouncement on these matters. What more do we know in this respect than the magicians of Ancient Egypt, the Puberty Officials of West Africa or even the pygmies of the dark equatorial forests? In spite of all our education and inherited culture, it is not always easy for us to rise above primitive ideas, as the most cursory glance at modern life and a daily newspaper will show. Human nature continues to be fundamentally primitive. But for the effect of environment and education, we would still be in the same state as the Bantus of West Africa who believe that the world is peopled with a crowd of spirits or the natives in Guina, where the sorcerers at spiritualistic meetings strictly forbid anyone to put foot to the ground as it would offend the spirits who are supposed to be swarming there.

Supernatural personification will not cover all the cases of primitive spiritualism or its counterpart to-day. I lean personally to the theory that spirits are really material, though unseen, many being simply influences, states of matter or impersonal forces.

The atmosphere is thus charged with spirit electricity or more probably with bacteria, although natural electrical forces are doubtless the cause of some of these perplexing problems. I agree with Dr. Crile of Cleveland when he says that the processes of the body are based on electrical phenomena and the growth and development of its functions are based on a definite series of radiations of various wave-lengths emanating from living substances in the body. These life rays, as they may be called, are ranged in all wave-lengths from ultra-violet to infra-red, and their activity is increased by such processes as malignant disease or narcotics.

As our knowledge of physics and chemistry increases, it is within the bounds of possibility that in the near future the presence of disease may be detected by the radiologist before it is outwardly apparent, and thus a tremendous advance will be made in prevention and cure.

I once knew an Austrian masseuse whose work formed a striking example of the life-ray theory. She advertised "electric massage" but the massage had nothing whatsoever to do with electricity as we understand it. It was generated in her body, and what was still more astonishing, it appeared to be under her personal control. Before the electric force or whatever it was became active, she closed her eyes and was apparently in deep concentration. Then some slight muscular tremors were perceptible, after which the battery was in complete working order. Her fingers could attract little bits of paper or other light objects as if they were a powerful magnet. She was usually somewhat exhausted after an exhibition of this kind, but the potential strength of the radiations had never diminished since her youth. At the time when I knew her, she was about fifty-five. She seemed to live in a universe of ethereal and invisible waves endowed with great energy.

I believe in the truth of such phenomena and that we do not yet know enough of the forces of nature to understand them. This has nothing whatsoever to do with attempts to get into communication with the spirits of the dead which, apart from its unwarrantable interference with the peace that they apparently desire, can cause so much physical and spiritual harm to the living. I knew a famous Italian doctor who always had the dinner table laid for his dead wife as if she were still alive and actually held long conversations with her at meal times. A carriage was also held in readiness for the deceased lady should she want to take a drive. Spiritualism leads to strange oddities in human behaviour now as in the past.

I have already referred to certain occult practices in

ancient Egypt, but the customs observed to-day are even more remarkable, for they prove that during the seven thousand years of Egyptian history there has been little change in the essential characteristics and pursuits of the inhabitants. The manners and customs and even the physiognomy of the people in Upper Egypt bear a striking resemblance to the Egyptians of the Pharaohs as revealed by ancient monuments and literature.

Nor has there been much change in their moral, material and intellectual conditions. Certainly during the last thousand years there has been little improvement in the social conditions of the people. Owing to the wide-spread poverty, what are known as deficiency diseases are greatly increasing; and for the same reason, there is a marked increase in crime, especially in the provinces. The vast majority of the people live under conditions which can only be described as revolting and a disgrace to the small minority who thrive and fatten on the miseries of others. While five per cent of the country is ruled on up to date and civilized lines, the remaining ninety-five per cent is still governed by antiquated laws and is in truth one of the most backward parts of the whole African continent.

The conservative instincts and natural docility of the fellaheen who work on the land from sunrise to sunset for about sixpence a day, may be partly responsible for this. These patient, hard working people after toiling all day under a scorching sun retire to hovels at night, hovels where they live with a varied assortment of animals and insects. I have actually seen enormous rats in one of these huts behaving as if all the place belonged to them.

The fellah, besides being patient and docile, is unfortunately unprogressive and a pronounced fatalist. This accounts for the survival of many strange customs founded on the primitive religion of the ancient inhabitants of the country. Some educated Egyptians who had studied in Europe have told me of their complete failure to impart their more progressive ideas even to their old friends who had never left the country. Some improvements have certainly been made of recent years but you still see in the fields exact reproductions of the scenes depicted on the wall paintings of the ancient monuments and temples.

The fellah, as we see him to-day, square shouldered, physically well developed, full lipped and with the familiar angular eyes, resembles the ancient labourer even down to the loin cloth or galabish. There is one difference, however, and it is an important one—he has a darker skin. It is a remarkable fact that the race, subdued again and again by the advancing hordes of Semites, Phœnicians, Persians, Greeks, Romans and Arabs, has been able not only to assimilate but also to fuse them into the common mould. It seems as if the soil of Egypt demanded one uniform stock and that the climatic conditions would tolerate no other. Although temporary racial variations may have sometimes appeared, there has always been a reversion to the original type which has remained obstinately Egyptian.

It is certainly a fact that foreigners die out after a few generations. I have been told that it is difficult to rear children except by the native methods. This seems somewhat questionable, considering the numbers of native children who die at a very early age from enteric fever or other similar affections.

The very soil seems to resent foreign interference. Some years ago modern ploughs and other agricultural implements were introduced but they were very quickly discarded. Thus you see to-day the same sort of plough drawn by two oxen that was used thousands of years ago. It lightly skims the surface and therein perhaps lies its advantage, for the soil of Egypt is different from that of other countries. Even foreign manures are not a pronounced success.

The shadoof with the workers in loin cloths and the shakieh with the blindfolded oxen which are both employed for raising water for irrigation purposes, are an exact counterpart of the methods of the Egyptians in the days of Moses. It is difficult to say which are most to be pitied, the labourers or the oxen. Food is still prepared in the same way and eaten with the fingers out of a common bowl, while water is poured over the hands before eating as depicted in ancient mural paintings. Flowers are often presented to each guest while seated at table. The water is then brought in jars similar to those used in the old days. They are manufactured in the same places and filled in the same way with leaves and flowers. The ancient form of greeting, touching the head and the breast, still continues. The dancing girls and singers are not so conspicuous as of old, but they clap their hands in time with the music in the ancient way. Even the scarecrows in the fields are adorned with the phallus as in the past.

One of the strangest and most terrible of the old practices still in existence is the dreaded Zaar, although it is prohibited by the Egyptian Government. I once had the rare privilege of witnessing this alarming performance through the influence of an Egyptian friend. The Zaar is a sort of rite of exorcism. Demoniac possession being considered the cause of much disease and infirmity, an attempt is made by exorcism to drive the evil spirits out of the victim and this performance is called the Zaar. The most unpleasant feature of the whole grim business is that the exorcists are not sheiks, fikis, witch doctors or even doctors of any kind but hideous old Sudanese women. There are generally six of them, four shekas and two bishops. And another curious thing is that the patients mostly come from the upper and educated classes. Women who have been educated in Europe and even the wives of Pashas have been known to undergo the cure, and what is more, they are cured even after years of illness and chronic invalidism. The cost of the cure is high, never less than fifty pounds and sometimes as much as two hundred and fifty.

The ritual followed is generally the same. In the centre of the room there is a large table heavily laden with fruit, vegetables, dead chickens, nuts, sweets of all kinds and alcoholic drinks. The first day is given up to exorcising the afreet or evil spirit which the patient firmly believes is in possession of her and is the entire cause of her ill health. The bishops play the most active part. They place their hands on the patient's head for several minutes and then speak some words of exhortation. When some music starts, the patient begins to dance first on one leg and then on the other. The musicians shake their tambourines and other instruments near her head and the patient gets more and more excited, dancing faster and faster until she becomes quite dazed and eventually drops to the ground in complete exhaustion. She seems as if she has been hypnotized.

There are various kinds of afreets, each requiring a different treatment. Or a patient may be possessed by more than one at the same time which necessitates a longer and more expensive treatment. Needless to say, this frequently happens.

While the performance is going on there is a terrible din and the air is thick with incense. It is enough to frighten any afreet away.

The two bishops must certainly be mediums, probably related to the Fikirs of the Sudan, although the methods which they employ for suggestion are different. The patient is also obviously under hypnosis throughout the performance.

All the good things at the table were nominally for the afreets to entice them away from their victim, but in reality most of them were consumed by the shekas. The second day's performance was largely a repetition of the first but it was more exciting and barbaric. Chickens were killed and their blood poured over the shekas and the unfortunate patient. Frequently goats and even camels were also killed and their blood likewise poured over the performers, while their meat always found its way to the houses of the astute old women. The ghastly performance reached its climax on the third day in a wild fantasia of music, dancing, exhortations, fumigations, eating and drinking.

I have been authoritatively told that it is very rare for a patient not to receive benefit from this unique treatment. There is certainly much general satisfaction among all concerned, the patient, her friends who form a sympathetic audience, the bishops, their assistants and it may be presumed the afreets who have so many good things provided for them, especially the British and Sudanese afreets who are always well supplied with whisky and booza respectively.

I do not know any country where there is more fuss made over weddings than in Egypt, and yet the marriage tie can be and is dissolved with the greatest rapidity. The laws relating to marriage and polygamy, the permission of concubinage and the facility of divorce are founded on the main principle of the constitution of Moslem society, that is to say chastity in both sexes before marriage. Moses allowed the chosen people, for the hardness of their hearts, to put away their wives and forbade neither polygamy nor concubinage. He who believes that Moses was divinely inspired to enact the best laws for his people, must consider the permission of such practices less injurious to morality than their prohibition among other peoples. On the other hand, many Europeans may consider such licence injurious both to morality and domestic happiness. But it probably restrains the profligacy of the people which would be far worse than anything existing in civilized countries. An Egyptian doctor once told me that there would be "no holding their women" without restrictive measures. He made no reference to the men, probably thinking it quite unnecessary, as anyone would agree from listening to the conversation among the men in any ordinary Egyptian cafe.

The Prophet knew his people, and although polygamy may not be observed as much now as in the past, there is ample justification for the practice inasmuch as he took to himself eight wives and married one of them, a child of ten.

The functions accompanying the marriage of a virgin are far more elaborate than those of a widow or divorced woman. Many marry at the age of twelve, some at the age of ten, but they are often betrothed two or three years earlier. In a recent census, there were a hundred and fifty-two husbands whose age was below ten years. And ten of these children had already been divorced while ten were widowers. The child brides are even more numerous. Six hundred and eighty married women were less than ten years old; thirty-seven had been divorced and seventy were widows.

As a rule marriages are arranged by a woman called a Khatbeh whose regular business it is. She makes a detailed report to the prospective bridegroom on the personal attractions of the young girls known to her and plays a very important part in the final selection. When the final choice has been made, a Khatbeh or a female relation is sent to the girl's friends to make her "wishes" known to them. If no objections are raised, negotiations are opened at once. The real fun begins when the amount of the indispensable dowry is discussed. The haggling with regard to this may last for days. One third is generally settled on the bride in case of the husband's death or the by no means remote possibility of an early divorce.

Parents may betroth their daughter to whom they please without her consent and marry her to whom they wish unless she has arrived at the age of puberty when she is supposed to have a say in the matter but seldom does in reality. The bridegroom never sees the bride until the time comes when she actually belongs to him. After the betrothal there are many ceremonies to be performed, such as the payment of the dowry, the signing of the marriage contract and the bride's bath.

Bridal processions to the house of the bridegroom are still to be seen every day in the streets but they are gradually losing their picturesque character, except perhaps in the provinces where the bride is still borne on a camel's back under a rich canopy. Marriages are also decreasing through a variety of causes, such as the greater freedom now allowed to young girls. The size of the procession depends on the wealth of the family, but unless a very poor one it is always headed by an Arab band including native bagpipes. Frequently Arabs may be seen marching through the streets carrying wardrobes, chests of drawers and other articles of furniture on their heads preceded by the inevitable musicians. These are the presents being paraded through the town.

When the great event is over and the bride has arrived in her new home, another ceremony takes place there. I attended one of these functions, a real one and not a bogus affair such as the dragomen arrange for the benefit of tourists. The bridegroom was entertaining his male friends downstairs. There was a plentiful supply of soft, sweet drinks, cigarettes and other refreshments. Recitations were given and there was singing of the most ear-splitting kind, although I was told that the singer was very famous and he was certainly loudly applauded after each of his songs. Upstairs the bride was entertaining some of her intimate female friends, dancing girls also being present. There are usually one or two of these

girls in the bridal chamber to entertain the happy couple
and to add to the gaiety of the scene on the first visit of
the bridegroom to his beloved, for this is the first time
that he has seen her and much depends on first impres-
sions. The old dayeh or midwife to the family is always
hovering about to report progress to the waiting crowd
of friends in the street. As soon as she appears at the
window and says that all is well, a loud demonstration
of joy takes place and the women utter shrill quivering
cries of delight.

These child marriages are a terrible blot on Egyptian
social life. It is surprising that some humanitarian
society has not agitated for the protection of these innocent little children. It is true that some Egyptian ladies
have recently raised their voices on their behalf, but
beyond fixing the age limit for marriage at sixteen (and
this is not observed) they have achieved little. Think of a
little girl of ten years of age, innocent as far as the
promiscuous life of her parents will allow, pretty, for
Arab children are usually handsome at that age, married
against her wish to a grown man. To make matters
worse, this man may have brutal instincts increased by
the regular use of noxious drugs, for it must be remembered that there are thousands of known drug addicts in
Egypt and that drugs are largely used under the mistaken
belief that they act as powerful aphrodisiacs. It is thus not
surprising that the prisons are full of murderesses drawn
from this youthful class. Many young wives are driven
by their husbands' brutality to seek an escape from their
sufferings by the only means of which they know—
poison. It is a terrible indictment of social conditions for
such tragedies to occur, especially as such unions, instead

of being forbidden, are actually sanctioned and approved by the current morality and religion of the people. It is right that murder should be considered an inexcusable crime, but one is almost tempted to excuse it in the case of these children considering their sufferings that force them to take such a desperate remedy. Anyone familiar with the barbarities inflicted on their poor little bodies must give way to feelings of sympathy and pity for them.

The Egyptians have very strange ideas with regard to childbirth. They believe that the health and appearance of the coming offspring depend on the objects seen by the mother before the child's birth. Thus the presence of a beautiful face at such times will ensure a beautiful child. To go to the other extreme, a monkey in the room might have disastrous consequences with regard to the child's appearance. The sources of such beliefs can be traced back to Genesis. Among the Copts, the bride may not go out even to see her parents until her first child has been born for fear of the malevolent influence of the evil eye which still permeates every phase of Egyptian life.

When the child is born its eyes are not opened as in Western countries. They are painted with a solution of coal tar and then sprinkled with kohl which is made by burning incense and almonds and collecting the soot. On the seventh day, the birth is celebrated. The rejoicings are always greater in the case of a son. In this respect the Arabs doubtless reflect the feelings of their ancestors who frequently destroyed their female offspring. This is the first time the child has a bath but if the parents are syphilitic, for some extraordinary reason, it is not touched until the end of the first year. If the child is not washed, a pot is filled with water and a piece of soap is lathered in it. In the centre of the pot, if the child is a boy, an abrig is placed. This is the big copper vessel commonly used for washing the hands. If it is a girl, the quallah, the ordinary vessel for drinking water, serves the same purpose. In both cases the vessel is decorated with the insignia of the respective sexes; a tarboosh, watch and chain for the boy and a handkerchief and ear-rings for the girl.

Three candles are placed round the rim of the pot. Parents and friends choose three names and each candle stands for a name. The candle that burns the longest gives the child its name. This custom proceeds from the mythology of ancient Egypt and the old belief that there are seven Hathors present at the birth of every child, for formerly seven candles were used but now only three. On the seventh night the midwife collects small quantities of cereals of every kind and places a portion of each in a pot. Other portions are stuffed into a small pillow and on this the child must sleep until old enough to distinguish his or her name. The remaining portions are tied up with a piece of cloth and placed under the mother's pillow. On the eighth day the child is placed in a large sieve like a corn sieve and the midwife makes a loud ringing noise with a pestle near the child's head, probably in an attempt to crush an afreet. At the same time she whispers wise injunctions into the child's ear, such as "Hear thy father's speech" or "Follow thy mother's advice", vigorously using the pestle with the obvious intention of standing no nonsense from any evil influences that may be about.

The abrig and quallah are next taken out of the pot and the water contained in them is sprinkled over the threshold of the room. Each of the guests snatches some of the nuts out of the pot and gives in return a piece of money to the midwife who carefully places it in her purse as a precaution against hard times.

A curious procession then takes place. All the children in the house assemble, holding lighted candles in their hands. The midwife leads the way with the child in her arms and cereals and salt wrapped in a cloth. The procession starts from the room where the child was born and visits all the rooms in the house in turn, chanting Arab hymns while the midwife scatters some of the grain in each room. The child is then given to the mother but she is not allowed out for forty days. During this time she is considered religiously impure and may not have a bath. This resembles the Jewish law that pronounces a woman unclean during forty days after bearing a male child and double that time after bearing a female. But perhaps its explanation is to be found in the astuteness of crafty and avaricious midwives.

Sterility is not recognized as due to any physical or physiological defect in Egypt but rather to occult causes. Remedies for it must therefore be obtained from supernatural sources.

A wife's reputation in her husband's eyes and in those of her friends and acquaintances depends on her fruitfulness. Barrenness in Egypt as elsewhere in the East is looked upon as a curse and a disgrace. A man seldom divorces a wife who has borne him children and without cogent reasons it is considered disgraceful to do so.

It is thus not surprising that childless married women resort to all kinds of devices to maintain their social standing as well as to retain their husband's favour. The cure of sterility has always been a favourite and profitable business for the charlatan. In the records of ancient Egypt there are constant allusions to the subject. The magicians played their part in accepted treatments of course but the gods also had a share in what was obviously a popular entertainment. Incubation sleeps in the temples were quite usual, with the recitation of appropriate spell and incantations. But it is difficult to understand how the appearance of a deity in a vision could produce the striking results so frequently recorded. To ascribe it all to suggestion is not entirely satisfactory as an explanation.

In the Cairo Museum there is a statue that has a very curious history, which throws some light on the mental stagnation of the people during the past two thousand years. It is dated 300 B.C. At that time there lived a priest named Zedher who enjoyed a great reputation for curing stings and snake bites and such ailments. To benefit his fellow men, he had the magical formula which prevented poison from taking effect engraved on the statue. When anyone had been stung, all he had to do was to pour water over the statue which then became imbued with the virtue of the formula. It was only necessary to scoop up some of the water running into a depression in the plinth and give it to the victim to drink to effect his cure. But Zedher was obviously unaware of the statue's potency as a cure for sterility. So successful has it been that the head has been worn quite smooth by the great numbers of Egyptian women who have rubbed themselves against it, and so great has been the rush to do so that a few years ago it had to be raised on a pedestal to prevent it from being worn away.

The Pyramids are also believed to have magic powers in this respect. Childless women will frequently visit one of them and walk round it seven times. But a far more alarming practice is that of a woman lying down between railway lines and letting a train pass over her. It is supposed to stimulate the circulation but fortunately it seems to be going out of fashion. Scarabs, the sacred beetles of ancient Egypt, are also dried, pounded and mixed with water and then drunk by women who believe them to be a sure remedy for failure to produce large families.

Other well known remedies include a visit to a cemetery, walking seven times round a dead body or stepping seven times over the water in which a corpse has been washed before burial. But no supposed cure for sterility is more curious or more unpleasant than a practice that was frequently adopted less than two generations ago. At that period there was a large open space to the west of the Citadel where criminals were executed. Persons convicted of capital offences were decapitated there. On the south of this place stood a building called Maghsil-es-Sultan or the Sultan's washing ground for the dead. There was a table of stone on which the decapitated person's body was laid to be washed before burial. There was also a trough to receive the blood-stained water that was never poured away.

Many women used to go there to obtain offspring or to expedite matters in the case of protracted pregnancy. They stepped over the stone table seven times with the left foot foremost and then washed in the foul water in the trough.

When a person is on the point of death in Egypt, the head is turned towards Mecca and when the spirit is departed there are loud cries of lamentation from the women folk and also from the public wailing women still very much in evidence especially in the country districts. I have often seen these women with their dishevelled hair uttering the most piercing shrieks. They throw dirt of any kind on their hair and carry a strip of blue linen or cotton which they wave to express their poignant grief. It is an emblem probably as old as the desert.

Funeral processions in Egypt are nearly all the same, the size and the loudness of the lamentations varying according to the wealth of the deceased. The advance guard of the procession generally consists of six or eight blind men called Yemeneeyeh who are symbolical of death. These paid mourners chant in a monotonous tone the usual profession of faith and other well known words from the Koran. They are followed by the male relatives, often riding on donkeys, also chanting in the same refrain. Then comes the open coffin simply covered over with a shroud and having some emblem on it signifying the sex or condition of the deceased. It is followed by the female relations riding in carts drawn by donkeys with the wailing women in the rear.

A curious feature of these funerals is that the bearers of the coffin do not proceed in a straight line but take a zig-zag course. The explanation lies in the supposed reluctance and resistance of the deceased to proceed to his last resting place.

Among the ancient Egyptians, no one could enter a

temple wearing a woollen garment and there was the same prohibition for the bodies of the dead. A similar custom prevails among the present inhabitants who generally wear cotton or cotton and silk mixed, while the dead are always wrapped in white and green cotton clothes.

During the war I was allowed two weeks' holiday and I went to what is called a rest house near the town of Dalmietta. On the first night after my arrival, a funeral took place. I was first made aware of it by a tremendous din in the streets, consisting of tambourines, kettle-drums and shrieking and wailing. Looking out, I saw the usual funeral procession but it was accompanied by innumerable dancers. There was no regularity or rhythm in the movements, each performer apparently assumed that she had the right to do what she pleased with her body and limbs. The result was a medley of ugly and irregular contortions. This awful death dance, for so it is called, with its hideous accompaniment of drums and cries lasted almost without interruption for three days and three nights. The din was so nerve-racking at times that I longed to go out into the desert and bury my head in the hot sand to escape from it. As far as I was concerned, the Dalmietta rest house was a dismal failure and I longed for the comparative peace of the noisy streets of Cairo.

Egypt is a land of paradox. Considering the people's inherent dread of cemeteries, their periodic ceremonial visits to the cities of the dead are difficult to understand. On certain days everyone goes to the local cemetery. A feast is held in the family vault and the greater part of the day and night is spent in the company of the dead rela-

tives. Each family has its own little house where the
dead are buried under marble slabs. This system is
peculiar to Egypt and is quite unknown in any other
Mohammedan country. It is thus doubtless one more
survival of ancient practices.

VI

MANY picturesque scenes and customs have disappeared from the streets of Cairo; some still remain, however, although sadly deprived of their former barbaric splendour. Not the least interesting are the processions accompanying the rite of circumcision. They are certainly unique, amusing and instructive. The visitors who see them from the terraces of Shepheards Hotel seldom have the slightest idea of their nature and significance, and when told about them in detail listen with an air of bewilderment and, as I have often experienced, indignation.

The rite of circumcision is not universally observed among the Moslem population. It is performed among them at the age of about five or six, or sometimes later. Among the poorer classes, there is usually a ceremonial celebration. Before the operation, the child is paraded through the streets, advantage sometimes being taken of a bridal procession to lessen the expense. The child generally wears a red Kashmeer turban or is dressed as a general or an admiral. In any case, he is gaudily attired. A handsomely caparisoned horse was formerly borrowed for the occasion but now the boy rides in an Arabieh or motor car. He is frequently to be seen holding a folded embroidered handkerchief before his mouth so as to hide part of his face. He does this to protect himself from the evil eye, salt being sprinkled behind him for the same purpose. The procession is generally headed by a jester performing tricks with a long pole, followed by the barber and his assistants carrying a symbolical sign called the heml, with the inevitable troop of musicians bringing up the rear. Some of the female friends and school-fellows of the hero of the day also walk in this curious procession. It generally starts from one of the mosques after the noon prayers. They visit their friends in the various parts of the city and are treated to sweet drinks and receive congratulations on the auspicious occasion. During the parade the most absurd ex-pressions are chanted, many of them being quite meaningless while others of course are in praise of the Prophet.

Among the Jews in Egypt the operation of circum-cision seems to be universally practised, and is always performed on the eighth day unless the child is ill when it is postponed for forty days. I once attended one of these functions. The father was an ex-British officer, a Christian, married to a Jewess. While the operation was being performed by a special man attached to the Syna-gogue for the purpose, the father held the child and the operator, who was very dexterous, mumbled some words in Yiddish which I was informed made the child irrevoc-ably a Jew.

But what is the history and origin of such barbaric mutilations, for barbaric they undoubtedly were, at least in their inception and intention?

It is impossible to affirm its existence in prehistoric times for obvious reasons. In historical times, in Egypt at all events, some assert that it was the general custom. But it is very suggestive that it is not referred to in any of the ancient manuscripts nor prescribed by any of the religious commandments. Only two representations of the operation have ever been found in Egyptian tombs, one in Sakkarah of the sixth dynasty and the other in one of the Theban tombs.

The word for circumcision in the Egyptian language means to purify, but whether this word is used in a ritualistic sense or as signifying personal cleanliness is extremely doubtful. It seems to have been obligatory among the priesthood at one time and then not to have been enforced with the same strictness, for in later times many uncircumcised mummies of priests have been found. Perhaps it lost whatever religious significance it ever had.

Some authorities assert that the laity alone were allowed to be circumcised and that this is proved by all the statues in the Egyptian Museums. Other authorities assert with equal confidence that all males in Ancient Egypt were circumcised. It is stated on the authority of Heroditus that the Egyptians were the first to introduce the rite from motives of personal cleanliness and that they then imparted their customs and ideas to neighbouring peoples.

It is one of the curiosities of Ancient Egyptian history that there is no substantial agreement between the various schools of thought on the most commonplace events. But after all, the difficulties are almost insurmountable, for how can a reliable history of a country be written from material found in tombs? Take two things like circumcision and trepanning for which the tombs are supposed to provide valuable data, it would be difficult to find two Egyptologists to agree on their position in

the life of ancient Egypt. If circumcision was so universally practiced as is suggested, why is there no reference
to it in any of the surviving texts, and why was it not
prescribed by the religious commandments? Again, how
is it that only two representations of the operation have
ever been found in the tombs or anywhere else? Considering the way that they chronicled the important
events of their lives, the omission is certainly remarkable. I would go further and say that in itself alone the
omission suggests that the operation was not universally performed and was not considered of any special
importance.

In the tomb of Ank-Ma-Hor at Sakkara where
it is represented the figure is a full grown adult
and the operation might conceivably have been performed for remedial reasons, especially when considered in connection with the words. The hiero-
glyphics are very significant and prove that the operation was performed by a priest. They may be translated
thus:

Priest: Hold tight lest he faints.

Assistant: Don't be afraid. Do what you want.

Priest: Good.

Assistant to the patient: He will cure you. The word
"cure" indicates that the operation was performed as a
remedy.

Egyptologists also tell us that the ancient Egyptians
were the most religious people known at the time. This
seems to me extremely doubtful. I can find no substantial
proof that the mass of the people were ever intimately
associated with the religious ceremonies and mysteries
which were far more probably confined exclusively to the

priests and their satellites. In later periods of their history, known events prove that little importance was attached to the rite of circumcision. In the nineteenth dynasty when the bonds that united Egypt with Nubia were broken, the Ethiopians looked on themselves as the sole orthodox representatives of the Egyptian religion. When the defeated nobles of Egypt came to do homage to the Ethiopian King, he only allowed one of them to enter his tent, for the others were uncircumcised and eaters of fish which was held in abhorrence by the Ethiopians.

I think it extremely probable that the rite of circumcision was religiously practised by the negroes at an early period and that it was actually introduced into Egypt by them. It is known that many negro slaves were then living in the country and that the natives were much impressed by the apparent sincerity of the negroes in their religious beliefs and practices. The African negro is peculiarly sensitive to religious influences and his loyalty to his gods is still a prominent feature of his life. We know that circumcision has been practised for more than five thousand years among the native tribes of the West Coast of Africa, and what is more that it is still practised to-day as universally as at any other period. Youths belonging to a few societies not practising it undergo the rite with novices of distant tribes and women, even old women, travel long distances to submit to the operation.

Considering all the evidence, this strange custom seems to have originated among the negro tribes in Africa, where for thousands of years it has never lost its religious significance. The Ethiopian negro monarch probably looked on the uncircumcised Egyptian nobles with the same abhorrence as some modern missionaries look on heathens and infidels to-day. At all events, in tracing the history of this curious rite among the negro tribes we are on firmer ground than by attempting to find its origin among mummified fragments or on statutes of the dead in Egyptian museums.

With regard to the Jews and their popular association with the rite from a religious point of view, historical evidence is neither conclusive nor satisfactory. A Jewish authority has informed me that the custom was taken from the Babylonians three thousand years before the Christian era. It is believed to have been introduced as a preventive of venereal disease said to have been very prevalent at the time. While the Jews gave the custom religious significance, it was gradually abandoned by the other native tribes and it thus became a distinguishing feature of the Jewish race. It is quite incorrect to say that Islam was responsible for the spread of the custom in Africa. It was extensively practised thousands of years before the introduction of the Moslem religion.

Further light has been thrown upon the administration of the law with regard to circumcision in ancient Egypt by the discovery of a number of papyri consisting of a rescript of the Emperor Antonionus. At that time, Egypt was a Roman colony and the edict was especially provocative, because not only the Jewish inhabitants but also all the numerous priestly families who worshipped the ancient deities had practised the rite of circumcision from time immemorial.

According to the Emperor's rescript, any medical man performing the operation was to be executed. Permission to do so could only be granted by the High Priest who resided at Alexandria. There were any number of formalities to be gone through, all providing unlimited opportunities for the time-honoured backsheesh; the rescript prohibited it for everyone except genuine Egyptian priests and Jews, the Emperor obviously not wishing to offend the powerful priestly hierarchy or the influential Jewish community.

Here is an extract from a papyrus dated A.D. 189:

"Wishing to circumcise my son, Pakebis, son of Cronion and grandson of Harpocration, a priest exempt from tribute; intended to succeed to the office of prophet in the temple; and also Paneses, son of my deceased maternal uncle. I pray you as usual to write to the great high priest in order to obtain authorization to circumcise these two children and accomplish the appropriate ceremony. This current year, Pakebis is seven years old, Panesis eleven. My husband, the aforesaid Cronian, is absent at Alexandria. He will bring them before His Highness the High Priest."

It is a curious fact that application to circumcise one of these lads, Panesis, appears to have been made two years before. For some unknown reason it was not granted, although the application was signed by four temple dignitaries.

Although sacerdotal kinship seems to have been essential for those wanting to be circumcised, it was not necessary for all members of the priestly families but only for those actually engaged in the cult of the gods, that

146

is to say ritual priests who personally approached the deity.

Finally the applicant had to present himself with his child at Alexandria. This was a most expensive matter for residents in Upper Egypt, but indulgence seems to have been sometimes granted as will be seen from the following letter:

"You are not ignorant of the anxiety I had in arranging the circumcision affair, but thanks to the valuable help of friends we have managed it."

The anxiety and trouble involved were indeed endless. The high priest at Alexandria considered the application and then examined the boys to see if their bodies bore any blemishes. Strange as it may seem, corporeal imperfection or blemish of any kind was considered a serious obstacle and only a jury of priests could decide on such a grave theological matter. It is easy to imagine the technical difficulties that must have arisen and the unconscious humour of the situation, considering that the Romans wanted to diminish the number of the operations. It must also have been a considerable source of income to the official class, for of course nothing could be done without backsheesh.

The origin of this strange custom is surrounded with as much obscurity as its history. It seems to have proceeded from a variety of motives. In the first place, it was probably considered hygienic and prophylactic. Then it was possibly connected with phallic worship and may be the surviving part of a prehistoric cult of human sacrifice. Or it may have been a sacrifice to the gods to preserve the rest of the body from harm. And finally, it may have been done in the belief that it promoted chastity. With regard to the Jews and the Egyptians, they differed from other nations in considering circumcision as a definite hygienic matter and a preventive of disease.

It has now been conclusively proved that it does not prevent disease and that there was probably no sanitary intention in its origin. When the fallacy of hygiene became prominent, it assumed a religious aspect in the primitive sense.

With regard to its possible phallic origin, it is noticeable that in the districts where the rite has been practised from time immemorial with the most elaborate religious ceremony, phallic societies have also flourished and continue to flourish to-day with the same secrecy and ritual. They are to be found along the West Coast of Africa and have a great influence, mostly for good, on the lives of the people. Membership is usually confined to males and the initiation is very strict. There is generally a man in command and a number of subordinates who rank as priests. Their decrees in all matters are final and unquestionable. Like Freemasonry, there are various grades and in most of the ancient societies progress is slow and precarious. There are ancient and elaborate purification ceremonies with the use of phallic signs, symbols and masks and sacrificial gifts to the gods of fertility. The rite has been practised with the same ritual for more than five thousand years and it obviously has a phallic origin. Some societies employ it as a primitive hygienic measure before marriage, but for the majority it has a phallic religious significance.

Certain practices among West African Societies prove that phallicism and circumcision are intimately connected. The Egbo and Nimm societies use the symbol of the tortoise, the emblem of motherhood and fecundity as ancient as the world itself. The former rules in South Nigeria and is extremely powerful. It is phallic and practises purification and circumcision. The Nimm rules extensively along the coast. It is one of the oldest of the religious cults and one of those that have been transplanted into the New World. Slaves from Nigeria have taken it to St. Domingo where it became the parent of the terrible Voodoo Society of Haiti and the other islands. The rites and signs include phallic survivals and circumcision. Some of the ancient signs can be seen in the mural decorations of the society's houses especially in the neighbourhood of Accra and Elmina.

The Humoi, influencing the Mende and other tribes in Sierra Leone, is a very old phallic society, retaining the tortoise as its chief sign, while its officials bear titles representing various phases of fertility. Both sexes are admitted at puberty. It practises purification, circumcision, the public whipping of offending women and sometimes of all the members of the family. But perhaps the most singular society in West Africa is the Kanda, an association of great age where the members are graded into septs or bands according to the year of their circumcision. In fact, it is impossible to get away from this strange custom, which is by no means confined to males, anywhere in Africa.

I have seen the operation performed at a mosque in Cairo where it is regularly done every Friday. The scene resembled a waiting-room in a public vaccinating clinic in England. Everyone seemed quite unconcerned about the whole proceedings. Although the methods adopted were very crude, I was told that ill effects were extremely rare.

VII

THERE are now very few drug addicts—among the tourist class—in Egypt, due no doubt in great measure to the energetic action of the Narcotics Bureau formed by Russel Pasha, the able Commandant of the Cairo Police, and also to the repeal of the iniquitous Law of Prohibition in America. The annual report of the Bureau is a most interesting and instructive document. The traffickers were of every nationality but they mostly came from the Balkans and Zurich where they had their headquarters. They were highly organized and it is really amazing how a few British Police officials have practically destroyed the whole drug traffic with all its ramifications in such a short space of time. The principal drug "Barons" were first arrested and convicted. It was discovered that they made enormous profits from a few successful coups and were living in the greatest luxury as a result. They wielded great influence and were said to be protected by persons occupying very high positions. For instance, I knew a chemist who was a notorious trafficker, well known even to the police. He had operated for years apparently with impunity. It was alleged that conclusive evidence had accumulated against him but for a long time nothing was done. He pursued his course calmly and serenely, strengthened by the knowledge that he had powerful men including pashas among his customers. But in the end the ingenuity and determination of the Bureau were too much for him and he paid the penalty for his many past and unpunished crimes.

Under the changed conditions, it is difficult to foresee what will happen. Now that the British will soon, it is feared, be withdrawn from control of the narcotics department, it would be somewhat optimistic to believe that the present satisfactory conditions will continue. I am inclined to believe that Egypt will again become a veritable El Dorado for the drug Barons. The prospects are far too tempting to be ignored by them. The majority of the large population in Egypt are only too willing to indulge in narcotics in the mistaken belief that they act as powerful aphrodisiacs. Even the fellaheen you see working in the fields must have his potion. It is not so easy to procure now and when they do succeed in obtaining it, it is usually adulterated and the price far beyond his means.

The fact of the matter is that the Egyptian, like the people of many Eastern countries, is fatally oversexed and is slowly but surely being burned to death by the fires of shameless lust, stimulated by artificial fuel by way of aphrodisiacs. This may be a serious statement to make but such an interpretation of the situation is supported by an examination of the divorce statistics. In 1898, they showed that out of every four marriages in Cairo, three ended in divorce. In 1926, they showed that for the whole of Egypt, there was one divorce for every twenty-four marriages. I am not concerned with the moral aspect of the matter but rather with its direct bearing on the rapid growth of the population and its sociological effect. It has been computed that if the population continues to increase at its present rate, and it certainly will do so unless divorce and child marriages are strictly regulated, the population will reach most alarming proportions in the next twenty years. At the present time it is estimated that five million people are either out of work or are dependent on others. In the big cities there are thousands of waifs and young vagabonds. For instance, Russel Pasha recently estimated that on the night of one police raid in Cairo there were a thousand juvenile vagabonds in the city. In his opinion, much of the filth and litter in the streets is caused by these children who in their search for food or profit pull the refuse out of the public dust-bins and sort it over.

This army of juvenile offenders forms a grave social problem and nothing very much is being done to ameliorate it. Millions are squandered on public buildings and vast sums are spent on marriages, circumcision, funerals and festivals but no one troubles about these hordes of starving children. But the real cause of the social disorganization and depravity in Egypt and the bad conditions that still exist undoubtedly proceed from the unrestricted use of drugs among the mass of the population. Even under the strictest supervision, the traffic in narcotics would be difficult to stop. The frontiers are so extensive, it is almost impossible to guard them properly. And then backsheesh is a factor that must never be forgotten, for it plays such an omnipotent part in the life of Egypt. In other countries it might be possible to stem this pernicious tide of narcotics but in a country where anyone will do anything for a tip, there is little hope of its suppression. You can never escape from demands for backsheesh in Egypt. It is the universal and all-powerful practice. By its means, there is ample proof that the dealers in drugs have even recently been able to obtain supplies sufficient for their purpose. Only a few years ago about half a dozen Egyptian doctors were convicted and imprisoned for supplying large quantities of drugs to their clients. I realized at the time of their trial what a great responsibility rests on doctors for creating in the first instance drug addicts by their prescriptions. More care is required in Egypt than anywhere else. In a country where dangerous drugs are easily procurable, young and unsophisticated people run more risks than in places where the traffic is either suppressed or controlled.

I remember a young and beautiful girl arriving in Egypt with her friends. After a few weeks her manner completely changed. She became taciturn and morose with occasional bursts of gaiety. I became suspicious but dared not tell her friends who were quiet and dignified people. So all I could do at the moment was to suggest that they should leave the country but the young lady was adamant in her refusal to do so and suddenly became intensely interested in Egyptian antiquities. Things went from bad to worse and I was finally compelled to tell her mother of my suspicions. She was terribly distressed but I managed to persuade her to do nothing and to leave me to solve the mystery. I consulted a British secret service agent with whom I had previously collaborated in some other delicate matters. I asked him to arrange for a watch to be kept on all the young lady's visitors. Nothing was said to the hotel staff because of the social position of the people concerned. After a few days I was informed by the police that an effendi had been seen acting in a suspicious manner on the terrace of the hotel. It was decided to keep a close watch upon him. The news did not in the least surprise me. I felt that a mystery which had caused great anxiety and worry was near solution. The next day the effendi appeared on the terrace again and was actually seen in close conversation with the young lady and to hand her surreptitiously a small package. Soon afterwards she developed the usual symptoms but in an even more aggravated form. After a consultation with the police, it was decided that I should wait for the arrival of this Egyptian which always occurred at the same time and ask for an explanation of his conduct. He arrived in due course. I told him that the young lady was ill (which was quite true) and asked him to give me anything that he had for her. He said that he had nothing and could not understand what I meant. I told him that he knew very well and would save a lot of trouble if he did what I asked. After a long argument, he handed me a small package whose contents I immediately recognized as cocaine. On that I kicked him down the steps from the terrace. To avoid a scandal no police action was taken and the young girl and her parents left for Europe as soon as possible. The mystery was solved but the question remained how this Egyptian effendi made the acquaintance in the first instance of this refined, dignified girl belonging to a family of high social standing? I have never been able to supply an answer, nor has anyone else. But a possible explanation suggests itself. Cocaine is an enslaving drug, most insidious and rapid in its conquest and most demoralizing in its effects. It is well known that victims of this drug take particular delight in dragging others down to their own level. This may have been the motive behind the scenes in this case.

In this connection, I have in my possession a prescription given to me by a doctor in Harley Street thirty-six years ago, with the remark—"Give that to your patients, it will tickle them up". It consisted of a spray containing 35 grs. of cocaine to an ounce of water. I did not understand it until years afterwards when I heard that he was a victim of the drug. The habit is easily acquired through nasal sprays, medicated drinks, sweets and throat lozenges. Medical opinion has often been invoked in favour of its use in cases of medical and bodily exhaustion. Cocaine has even been prescribed as a substitute and cure for morphinism. One can only think of the man out of whom one devil was cast and went and took unto himself seven other devils worse than the first.

My next example is somewhat different from the last. I was once called to see two young good-looking girls at an hotel. They were victims of alcohol and consumed vast quantities of it every day. They were put under the care of a nurse. I soon learned that they frequently received two young Egyptians who were said to be members of very ancient families. I was told that they therefore deserved to be treated with every consideration and respect. But I knew only too well that noble lineage is often claimed by a certain type of the effendi class with great wealth of detail and plausibility. Such stories never fail to take effect on high-spirited, unsophisticated young girls, especially if they are Americans. As far as I could see, the only sign of noble lineage in many of these effendis was their strict adherence to certain primitive tribal customs. They went about in their homes barefooted, wore galabicks and squatting on the floor consumed vast quantities of food from a common dish using nothing but their fingers. When I found that my patients were receiving objectionable visitors, I gave strict orders that they were not to be admitted to see them. I soon learned, however, that my orders were indignantly resented and also that they had dismissed a previous doctor who had objected to these visitors. I spoke to the young Egyptians and threatened to see the American Consul about the matter. In their indignation, they had the effrontery to say that they were only trying to save the Sitts (young ladies). I appealed to the manager of the hotel and he prohibited them from going upstairs, but they bribed the servants and succeeded in eluding our vigilance. We cut off all supplies of alcohol as far as we possibly could and as soon as they had sufficiently recovered, I dispatched them in charge of a nurse to join their steamer at Alexandria. They left without attempting to conceal their dislike of me, a feeling undoubtedly shared by the members of the ancient families. I was quite satisfied at having aroused such resentment, well knowing that I had saved them from themselves although they did not appreciate it.

On another occasion I was asked to interfere in the case of a young girl belonging to a most respectable family who was being considerably annoyed by the attentions of a young Egyptian. The acquaintance had begun in Upper Egypt and beyond ordinary politeness on her part, there was nothing to explain his persistence. He thought that he was deeply in love with her and did not see any objection to the marriage that he intended, for after all he belonged to an ancient family and his father possessed a thousand feddans of land which he would in due course inherit. I saw that it was no use talking to him, for he belonged to the insolent, dark, Arab type, but when he was seen loitering about next time near the girl's house, a police officer was there to meet him. He told him that there was a train leaving for Luxor at a certain time and that he would be there to see him off by it. Sure enough he left by that train; all his braggadocio, courage and transient lust had vanished through his tarboosh.

This undesirable type of young man is certainly on the increase. It partly proceeds from the absurdity of the school system. The students lack all discipline and no serious attempt is made to develop their characters. The system is an intellectual hothouse unfavourable to common sense. It causes mental and nervous strain which often shows itself in aberrations of this sort intensified by indulgence in hashish or other narcotics.

I once received an urgent message to visit a young lady taken suddenly ill in the desert. I gladly went for it seemed to provide me with an entirely new kind of adventure. Shortly after passing the Great Pyramid, our car broke down and we had to return to Mena House and telephone to Cairo for another. As we were waiting, I anxiously wondered what was happening in the desert. At last we started again for our unknown destination, for no one knew where the young lady's camp exactly was. It was now nine o'clock at night, blowing hard and bitterly cold. When we got well into the desert, the wind amounted to a raging gale. In the darkness, it was almost impossible to keep to any sort of course across the sand. At midnight my two Arab companions were standing with me beside the car having almost decided to return as it seemed quite hopeless to attempt to proceed, when I suddenly saw a light. I went towards it and found two girls camped with the usual dragoman escort. The younger girl said that she had had a heart attack but I could not find much the matter with her and certainly not enough to warrant my staying there for the night, especially as I had a bad case waiting for my attention in Cairo just then. So I decided to return. It was a most unfortunate decision, for it nearly cost me my life and, a minor consideration, the goodwill of my patient and her friend.

Shortly after starting on the return trip the car broke down. I asked the dragomen how far it was to the Great Pyramid. He replied without any hesitation that it was about half an hour's walk. Very foolishly and quite against all experience of dragomen and their trustworthiness, his word was accepted. The wind was very cold and it blew the sand in one's eyes, ears, nose and mouth so that one felt almost suffocated. We walked or rather crawled slowly along. We reached a mound of dry sand and were delighted to see the Pyramids apparently quite close at hand, but on descending on the other side they completely disappeared from view, and we had laboriously to plough our way through the soft sands before reaching the next mound. This phantasmagoria continued for hours and I fainted several times and should never have survived if it had not been for a flask of Irish whisky which I fortunately had with me. Our three worst dangers were suffocation by the sand, the intense cold and the terrible desert thirst.

I repeatedly begged one of the Arabs to go to Mena House for assistance but he absolutely refused to do so. He said that he was afraid of being eaten by hyenas or wolves. After that, whenever I saw a tuft of weeds waving in the wind or a large stone, I thought it was a voracious animal. The Arabs told me, however, that hyenas and wolves only attack a man when he is alone, never when accompanied by one or two others which I believe is correct. At last, thoroughly exhausted, semi-conscious and semi-delirious we eventually reached Mena House after five hours of hard struggling, an unquenchable thirst being one of our greatest difficulties. I never saw my patient in the desert again but I heard of her and her friend. They both belonged to wealthy families and they did not err on the side of generosity as far as I was concerned.

I came across one remarkable case of chronic morphinism in which the habit had undoubtedly been contracted in the first instance by the unwise use of the drug by one of her doctors. Indeed, judging from what she told me, at one time at least morphia had been wilfully and intentionally employed. She was an elderly lady, the daughter of a man with an international reputation, and a very brilliant woman in her lucid moments which regularly lasted for three weeks in every month.

Many years before she had been told by a doctor that she suffered from a disease of the fifth nerve and what she did not know about "Trigeminus", as she always called it, was not worth knowing. When she complained of the slightest pain in the face, out came the syringe (and like a doctor I knew in Cairo, her method of sterilizing the needle was to draw it between her lips). She naturally suffered from facial pain very frequently.

When I saw her I was convinced that she was not suffering from "Trigeminus" at all but to make sure I called in an eminent surgeon in consultation. He most emphatically agreed with me and suggested that radical measures were quite uncalled for.

I tried other drugs as palliatives for the imaginary pain but she had reached the stage when she could tell the drug used by the sensation it produced. All that one could do was to make her life as tolerable as possible and to protect her from herself as far as one could, for her emotional nature was as strong as it was unbalanced. She imagined that she was in love, no doubt not for the first time, but on this occasion the unhappy victim of her unwelcome attentions was a very famous and distinguished man. The situation reached such a pitch that he hurriedly chartered an aeroplane and told the pilot to fly as fast as he could until he reached the frontier. Just as he was taking off, the lady arrived at the aerodrome. In her excitement, she offered large sums of money for a plane to go in pursuit of her imaginary lover. Fortunately no one accepted her offer and the poor lady died shortly afterwards a physical and moral wreck. Thus ended what might have been a brilliant career, but in spite of everything she remained a most lovable woman to the last, always generous and helpful to the needy.

Another case comes into my mind of a kind and lovable person who incurred the drug habit through the fault of a doctor far too ready to alleviate even the slightest pain with his needle. When I first saw this man in his hotel in the early hours of the morning, he was in a terrible state and I soon realized that there was nothing for it but to give him an injection of morphia. I had only just returned to my home when he arrived craving for more. I refused but when in despair he threw himself on the ground and kissed my boots pleading for more, I had to give in. After this second dose, he seemed comforted. In two or three days by giving him gradually diminishing doses, he became almost normal and remained so for about a month. Then the uncontrollable craving for the drug once more asserted itself and for some days he was a veritable maniac.

The most extraordinary thing about this man was that he travelled round the world visiting various countries in connection with his business which thanks to his activities was always most successful. He was passed on from one doctor to another in the various cities of various countries. Every three years he turned up in Cairo with his habitual smile and his demand for his usual treatment.

My next case of this kind gave me perhaps more worry than I have ever experienced and that is saying much, but the lady in question was worth it as she had many excellent qualities. She was the victim of circumstances, one of which was the possession of more money than is good for anyone to have and being a lovable and generous person she was inevitably surrounded by the usual crowd of false friends. She arrived in Cairo with a nurse and another companion who acted as a general factotum and immediately began drinking to excess. I inspected the bar bill and found that in one day fifty-two cocktails had been consumed, besides whisky, beer and champagne. Orders were given not to supply so much liquor but there was nothing for it except to let matters take their course. Illness finally compelled her to go into hospital and I hoped that she would benefit from the absence of her attendants whose influence was so injurious. Indeed one of them was discovered unconscious in the desert with an empty bottle beside her. Things went on smoothly in hospital until one day she asked me and some others to join her at a tea party in a café. When it was over, I put her into a taxi and told the driver to go to the hospital. Late that night I received a telephone message from the matron asking me what had happened to my patient for she had never returned. After a long search, I at last found her in a deplorable condition. She was not allowed out again and instructions were given that her companions were not to be admitted when they called to see her. A long and arduous struggle ensued. Finally I prevailed upon her to accompany me to Europe on the excuse that she should try the cure at a certain spa but in reality to get her away from her undesirable companions. Later on I got in touch with some of her friends in America and they came to Europe and took my patient back with them. She lived a few years longer and died peacefully and happily surrounded by real friends who appreciated her many good qualities.

The worries and anxieties of a medical practitioner in a tourist centre are many and varied. Difficult and sometimes amusing situations are always arising. On one occasion I was called out of bed in the early hours of the morning in January when the cold in Egypt is intense to see a lady who was said to be very seriously ill. When I arrived at her hotel, I found a lady sitting up in bed in immaculate negligée looking the picture of robust health. The floor was strewn with scores of letters. Before I could ask her what was the matter, she said in an imperious manner: "Read those letters". I told her that I felt it hardly belonged to a doctor's duties to read other people's correspondence, but in order to satisfy her I picked up some of the letters and glanced at them. They were obviously love letters, bristling with passionate declarations. I again asked her what was the matter. She replied very impressively: "Here I am in Egypt where we had arranged to be married and now he has turned me down". I protested that I was helpless in the matter and advised her to leave a climate notoriously dangerous for anyone unable to control his emotions. She was very indignant and showed her displeasure by refusing to pay my fees when an account was presented to her next day. She did not even take my advice but stayed in Cairo and called in another doctor who no doubt was only too willing to read her love letters.

Shortly after this experience I was urgently called to see a young lady seriously ill at Shepheards Hotel to which I was attached in an unofficial way as the doctor called upon in most emergencies. A lady was travelling with her two daughters and one of them had been taken suddenly ill in the early hours of the morning. I was kept waiting for some time outside the bedroom door and then the mother appeared and said that my services were not required as her daughter was better and with that she unceremoniously closed the door. I said nothing about my fees then, for I have a rooted objection to mentioning them when visiting a patient but my account was rendered in due course. Now these people were occupying expensive rooms in the hotel but they left Cairo without attempting to settle their account with me, doubtless thinking that because I had not actually attended the lady in question there was no need to do so. They completely ignored the fact that I had been called from my bed on a cold wintry morning at their request and thus required and deserved some compensation. It is usually the people with the most money who are the most inconsiderate in their treatment of the medical advisers.

Not long after this I had another night or rather early morning call. I was ill at the time myself and had a high temperature when I received an urgent message to go at once to Shepheards Hotel to see a gentleman very seriously ill indeed. Temperature or no temperature, I have never declined a night call and on this occasion I was delighted that I had not hesitated to take the risk, for I should otherwise have missed one of the most humourous situations that I have ever witnessed.

There were two beds in the room into which I was shown. One of them was occupied by a forbidding look-ing woman who was apparently engrossed in a book that she was reading. She just raised her eyes for one second as I entered and said good morning and then she returned to its pages with even greater interest. Pacing the room was a man in a very elaborate dressing gown with a black skull cap on his head. Apart from the first greeting, not a word was spoken. The woman went on reading and the man continued his march up and down the room and neither of them paid the slightest attention to me. So I sat down unasked and patiently awaited developments with some amusement.

At last the patient stopped walking up and down and looking straight towards me said very slowly and deliberately: "Doctor, I have had a headache for the past two or three days and I thought it was time to see some-one about it." I told him to go to bed and gave him some tablets from my bag, promising to give him some special remedy for his headache later, which I did by sending him an account with the maximum fees for a night call. To my surprise, it was paid with thanks.

Later on in the summer I was reminded of this incident by another amusing situation of a somewhat similar kind. I was staying at the historic Hotel Villa d'Este on Lake Como for a few days as the guest of the proprietors. On leaving I caught the early morning boat for the other end of the lake. On the pier there was an American lady very intently reading a book while her husband strolled about. She never raised her eyes from its pages and when she got on board the steamer she sat down and continued reading completely oblivious of everything and everybody around her. After about two hours she turned for a moment to her husband and said: "Say, Sam, is this Lake Como?" Sam replied: "Sure, Saidie, they call it a lake but I guess we'd call it a duck pond in the States." This information apparently conveyed nothing to Saidie for she went on reading even while Sam was still speaking. It was a perfect morning and she was surrounded by some of the most beautiful scenery in the world, but doubtless to her it only meant that she had traversed a few more miles of the earth's surface and could boast to her friends of having done so.

The most curious example of unnecessary night calls that I have heard of was related to me by Dr. Douglas Mackay some years ago. A doctor was called out on a dark wet winter's night to go to a distant cottage on an unapproachable hillside in the country. On arrival, he asked the people what was the matter. He was told that their daughter had been in bed since she was five years old with a tuberculous spine and that the previous doctor had said she must be watched carefully when she reached the age of twenty-one. It was her twenty-first birthday and they added in explanation of the urgent call, "as she was born at a quarter to two in the morning, we thought you'd better see her."

This story may seem improbable but I am quite sure that quite as curious and far more aggravating calls are being made on doctors in Great Britain to-day. For many of them, they get no remuneration. There is some truth in the definition of panel doctors as the only members of the medical profession who are paid for their services.

A practitioner is also faced with other difficulties of an entirely different kind. I was once asked by a very well known man in the political world to go at once to see a lady who he said was seriously ill. On arrival, I found a young girl almost in extremis. Her condition was so critical that I asked no questions but a superficial examination strengthened my suspicion that she had had a miscarriage, although there were no objective indications usual in such cases. She gradually recovered in spite of great mental anguish which it was pitiable to witness.

Now the question arises, should I have reported the case to the authorities? In my opinion, I did right in minding my own business which was that of making her well and getting her away from Egypt, leaving moral and judicial matters severely alone.

About the same time, I was faced with another moral problem. I received an urgent call to go to a young girl who had attempted suicide and had very nearly succeeded. She had apparently had a liaison with another well known politician, this time a Pasha. As she was a native of a country in central Europe, I simply informed her consul and left her in his charge.

During the revolution of 1919 in Egypt, there was a very serious situation in Cairo for several months. The city was without electric light and gas. There were no servants, tramcars or taxis, in fact it was a general strike in its very worst form. In addition, British subjects had to endure all kinds of annoyances and insults, not only in the street but also on the telephone. As is well known, several prominent men were assassinated.

I visited my hospital in Shubra where I acted as Medical Superintendent every morning without any trepidation but I fortunately took the precaution of telling the Matron to have the telephone number of the military picket in a conspicuous place in case of emergency. Such an occasion did arise. On the morning when the trams began to run after a stoppage of three months, the first to pass the hospital suddenly stopped. There were two young British soldiers on it, one in front and the other behind. I saw them descend into the street obviously much perturbed. There was a good deal of shouting and I could see some four hundred Arabs some distance away approaching the soldiers in a very threatening manner. I immediately went out to their assistance. I asked one of them if he were a good shot and he nervously replied in the affirmative. I pointed out the leader of the mob and told them to point their rifles towards the crowd but not to fire until I gave the order to do so. I refrained as long as seemed advisable but eventually said: "Fire!" again directing their attention towards the leader, a powerful looking fellow who was brandishing a big stick. He fell to the ground mortally wounded. I again told them to point their rifles at the crowd which momentarily halted but not to fire until I gave the word.

Meanwhile the armed picket drove up and without doubt saved our lives. The crowd, however, shortly afterwards attacked the Greek conductor of the tram and I had the greatest difficulty in rescuing him but only after he had received terrible scalp wounds that necessitated his removal to hospital for treatment.

The only injury that I received in this skirmish was to my new suit of clothes which was saturated with the tram conductor's blood. The soldiers were afterwards summoned to appear before a Court Martial for shooting the Arab. A friend of mine who served on the inquiry told me afterwards that when asked for an explanation, one of them said that a gentleman, apparently a doctor, had come to their assistance and told them to fire like hell. Needless to say from the above description, this was not quite accurate.

When I had the body of the Arab removed to Hospital, I failed to find the entrance or the exit of the bullet.

After those tragic and disastrous years when men's minds were filled with enmity and doubt and many cruel assassinations took place, it is a great joy to witness the present happy relations between the two countries. Not only have all traces of bitterness been removed but the closest friendship and confidence have now been established which forms a happy augury for the future.

The worries and annoyances inseparable from a doctor's life in places frequented by the travelling public (which is not always the best part of the population by any means) are indeed interminable. I have already alluded to the types enslaved by drugs and alcohol and to the selfish contemptible people who have no consideration for the feelings or interests of their medical adviser. But I came across an even more objectionable type in the tourists who camp in the desert with low class natives, paying exorbitant sums for the pleasure of their society. White women lose the respect of the natives when this sort of thing is allowed to go on, and the result is that decent women cannot walk in the streets without being molested. In the case of British women, an appeal to the Consul usually results in their deportation but in the case of others, you might as well whistle for the wind as try to do anything in the matter.

VIII

A TRIP to the Sudan in the month of May is not an excursion which many people would choose for themselves. However, when one of my patients in Cairo asked me if I would accompany an expedition of which he was the head, I accepted his invitation. I did not learn of the object of the expedition until we reached Khartoum. It was to make fuel from papyrus and oom suff (or mother of wool) to be found in the Bahr Gazal district, a desolate swamp, perhaps the most desolate part of the world. It covers an area of thirty-six thousand square miles. There is nothing to be seen in it but reeds, the most voracious mosquitoes to be found anywhere and an occasional whale-beak stork, the most melancholy and forlorn looking bird in existence.

The immense area consist of a series of swamps and lagoons with several rivers whose channels are constantly changing owing to the movements that are continually taking place in the Sudd. Throughout the vast region, the water is very shallow and moving masses of Sudd make it very dangerous. They resemble ice packs and travellers are often blockaded by them for weeks on end. Violent storms and torrential rains are frequent at certain times and these, coming on earlier than was expected, caused great damage to the equipment of the expedition and all operations had temporarily to be suspended. While I was there, we were content to make general observations and collect specimens of the various seeds for scientific investigation afterwards at Khartoum. Briquettes were subsequently made but as far as I know the only combustion process that resulted was the conflagration caused by the burning of other people's money.

I remember at the time meeting in Cairo a well known man, a patentee of a much advertised milk. He asked me for my opinion of the scheme. I replied that I was so busy in the Sudan shooting crocodiles, elephants and game of every description that I was interested in nothing else. However, I added that I thought it would be more feasible and perhaps more commercially profitable to utilize in some way the calorific powers of the sun in that country than to experiment with the papyrus and oom suff on what appeared to be a purely hypothetical basis. This process was, I believe, tried by an American company both in the Sudan and Egypt but proved a failure also.

It is of melancholy interest to recall now that the highly respected Sir Lee Stack who was afterwards assassinated, was, to my personal knowledge, a firm believer in the Sudd scheme.

Khartoum is a disappointing place. Apart from the official residences magnificently and lavishly laid out and a few Greek bars and grocery shops, there is not much else. Wide embryonic streets are still waiting for houses to adorn them. They will have to wait a long time. Neither white men nor industry could thrive in that awful summer heat. During the ten days we spent there making preparations for the trip, the temperature ranged from between one hundred and twenty and one hundred and twenty-five degrees Fahrenheit in the shade, and in addition we were treated to one of those infernal dust storms called haboubs. This particular one came from the South and in a few minutes day was converted into night. The sand penetrated everything so that men and beasts were compelled to throw themselves on the ground and press their faces against the earth in their endeavours to escape the suffocating dust. To make matters worse, the haboub was followed by torrential rain accompanied by thunder and lightning.

These storms have a most deleterious effect on the health. They generally occur about nightfall, so that neither rest nor sleep is possible. Both food and drink are covered with infected dust. It is not surprising that those compelled to live in such places suffer from nervous irritability. But from what I observed in Egypt and some tropical places, I am convinced that ill health is not entirely caused by the climate. I would rather say that the insane and inane pursuit of exercise at all cost and at all times, together with other inordinate indulgences, were the prime cause of ill health in the East. It is certainly an amazing sight, much commented on by foreigners, to see apparently sane Englishmen playing strenuous games in a blazing sun with the atmosphere heavily laden with sand and the temperature varying between one hundred and five and one hundred and twenty-five degrees Fahrenheit. They say that they can only "keep fit" in this way, totally disregarding the most elementary laws regulating health. Such views amount to what is positively an obsession with the most tragic results in many cases. Military doctors have told me that much illness among the troops in hot countries is due to exhaustion and chills after games, thus placing altogether unnecessary burdens on the unfortunate taxpayer.

The relative value of exercise has always been a matter of dispute. There is no subject connected with hygiene which men are so prone utterly to neglect or to run to the most absurd extreme. Personally I have no sympathy whatsoever with violent exercise of any shape or form when carried out under a tropical sun in an atmosphere laden with infected dust. Instead of promoting rational physical development, it has precisely the opposite effect.

Greek and Roman history provides many examples of the extremes to which nations as well as individuals will go in their attempt to achieve perfect health and a fine physique. The physicians of the period fully realized the dangers of excessive exercise and expressed their opinions with extreme frankness. For instance, Hyppocrates declared athleticism contrary to nature and condemned gymnastics as they were then practised. Galen said that the athlete's training not only predisposed him towards disease but actually caused him to contract it.

It is, of course, essential to distinguish between physical exercises and sports in which the prime object is to excel over others. It is these sports which are often inimical to health from the medical point of view. They also actually cause abnormalities in the human body. For instance, the fencer has his right quadriceps abnormally developed with a resultant clumsy swelling on the right thigh. The Basque players of pelota, notoriously short-lived people, have hypertrophied forearms and deltoids. Acrobats look like monkeys with over-developed shoulders, retracted abdomens and arched backs. As for the devotees of that extraordinary modern craze, golf, the female of the species develops hands and feet that would shock our mothers.

I have no wish to condemn rational exercise but only exercise when it is carried to excess, especially under the blazing sun of tropical countries. The question mainly resolves itself into the matter of how much food and drink is consumed in hot climates. The individual who overeats and drinks too much alcohol must likewise take too much exercise so as to get rid of an excess of waste products; but those who eat and drink moderately need not exercise in this way, and the less they do under such conditions, the better for their bodily health. The ancients were very accurate observers with regard to the effect of physical exercises and can be called upon to support the above views. They were well aware that those who specialized in sport were unable to endure the fatigue of war as well as their more ordinary fellow soldiers. They noticed that such men had no real endurance, were temperamentally unbalanced, became senile before their time and died prematurely. Anyone considering the question with impartiality must agree that the excessive illness and high mortality among British residents, civil and military, in warm countries is largely due to excessive indulgence in games and sports. To this might be added, perhaps as a natural consequence of such undivided attention to sport, neglect of hygiene. For instance, in Egypt the hygiene of the kitchen is left to the mercies of Berberines, flies, mosquitos and other insects.

Much might be learnt on the subject from a study of the habits of animals. Compare the short lives of such restless active animals as cats, dogs and horses to the almost incredibly long lives of the animals who take things quietly. The parrot who rarely leaves his perch lives well over a hundred years. The elephant does the same if left unmolested while the allotted span for the lazy tortoise runs into hundreds of years.

At the present time, many people seem to react automatically to the predetermined stimulus of the fetish of exercise, as the top responds to the boy who whips it. The race would be healthier if there were more mental activity of the right sort and less slavish subservience to games and sports and the endless, monotonous, senseless discussion of their merits and demerits. If this digression requires excuse, it must be the memory of several people playing strenuous games in Khartoum when the temperature was one hundred and twenty degrees Fahrenheit in the shade.

But I have another recollection of Khartoum of a much more pleasant nature. I had read with considerable trepidation of the ravages of the mosquito there only a few years previously. One writer confesses that he was driven to go and stand in the Nile up to his neck to escape the attentions of these voracious pests. I was simply amazed by the progress that had taken place in the control of this scourge. I was told that if one were seen in a habitation, it was actually an offence and the householder could be fined.

On the other side of the Nile is the large native town of Omdurman. A good deal of trading seemed to be going on in that evil-smelling furnace when I was there. The only object that impressed me was the dilapidated tomb of the once dreaded, powerful and ferocious Mahdi. The tomb had been dismantled by the orders of Lord Kitchener but I do not believe that the popular legend of the body being thrown into the river, also by his orders, is correct. Lord Kitchener did not hesitate to run counter to the revered, traditional ideas concerning saints when it suited his purpose, as will be realized from the following incident.

All over Cairo can be seen tombs of saints which must never be demolished or disturbed in any way. One of these occupied a prominent place in the Station Square on a site which Lord Kitchener wanted for a barracks for the British Military Police. The Egyptians absolutely refused to give permission for the tomb to be moved elsewhere. Great was the consternation when the sacred coffin was found one morning in Shubra, a neighbouring suburb. Inquiries were made and the Saint was reported to have said that the noise in the Station Square was too much for him and that he wanted to rest in a more peaceful place. Hence this apparently miraculous transportation which the Egyptians acclaimed as proof of their Saint's powers, little imagining that a party of British soldiers had acted as agents for the unseen world. A new mausoleum was erected for the Saint in Shubra, while a new building was built on the old site for saints of another order.

But K. of K., as he was called by all the British officials in Cairo, was looked upon as a god who could do no wrong. It was most amusing to observe the awe which he inspired among them. If one timidly asked what he had done to deserve all this obsequious reverence, a look of pitiable contempt was the only answer one got. And yet it was quite a justifiable and reasonable question, as was proved by subsequent events.

I was once a member of a deputation that went to Lord

Kitchener to ask for a government subsidy for the development of tourism in Egypt. We got little satisfaction. He said that the people who profited by the tourists were the hotels and the tourist agencies and that it was thus for them to pay for any further development. This was an extremely narrow and mistaken point of view, as a glance at the policy of governments everywhere to-day will show. He used to preside regularly at the big Irish dinners in Cairo on St. Patrick's Day, making speeches to which even the most nationally-minded Irishman could not object. And yet his policy at the outbreak of the war towards Southern Irishmen was one of the biggest mistakes ever made by a responsible man, as Lloyd George himself has stated. It led undoubtedly to the Easter rebellion and exasperated the enmity that existed between two peoples who should have co-operated for the common good.

The Southern Irishmen, treated with disdain and refused commissions, replied, so to speak: "Very well, you refuse to let us fight for you, then we will fight against you." Their attitude was only what might have been expected and should have been foreseen.

During our stay in Khartoum, I was fortunate enough to meet Father Ohwalder of the Austrian Mission. He told me a little about his terrible experiences while a prisoner of the Mahdi and subsequently of the Khalifa. I can still picture this unobtrusive, self-denying man in his little mud church surrounded by his faithful negro followers in a district where the smells are suffocating.

The historic slaughter known as the Battle of Omdurman took place some distance from the native town. Traces of it are still to be seen in the way of bones and skulls lying about. It is impossible to get away from human remains in Egypt and they are considered with as little concern as if they belonged to a hyena or other wild animals.

The trip up the White Nile was in many respects pleasant but the heat was terrific and in consequence our thirst insatiable. I do not know any suffering more excruciating than the intense desert thirst experienced in the Sudan and Egypt especially under a summer sun. It cannot be assuaged. When fluid is swallowed, it pours out almost instantaneously through the pores of the skin. So far as fluidifying the blood is concerned, it is almost valueless.

The scenery in the White Nile area is more diversified than in Egypt. There are extensive plains, woods, hills and much vegetation, while mountains are sometimes visible in the distance. One of the most interesting sights that I have ever seen was the multitude of birds in the early morning after leaving Khartoum. There appeared to be millions of them, mostly of great size, and many standing on one leg like the Dinkas and Shilluks further south. We also encountered some crocodiles. I shot at some of them but only succeeded in securing one, a huge monster, which fell to my rifle at a distance of about five hundred yards. There was great excitement among the natives who quickly arrived in crowds from their villages. As they all wanted a special tit-bit, it was with difficulty that they were prevented from eating each other.

It is extraordinary how quickly the savage spirit shows itself among primitive tribes everywhere, especially when food is concerned. But, after all, the same greedy propensities may be seen among many so-called civilized people, only they are usually concealed under a thin cloak of politeness.

Hippopotami were also very numerous. In one stretch of the river, I counted as many as thirty-seven disporting themselves along the mud banks. I wondered how they managed to grow so fat in such a wilderness. Elephants and monkeys were also to be seen in great numbers. The Sudan is still the habitat of the dog-faced ape, one of the most intelligent of his species.

It was very interesting to observe the distinct characteristics of the various tribes along the river. These were shown even by the formation of their huts which were in every way superior to those in Egypt. The conditions of native life are far worse there than anywhere else. Curiously enough the further south you go after leaving Assuan, the better the habitations and the cleaner the villages.

Although the Dinkas and the Shilluks are only separated by the river, they are as different as the Portuguese and the Swedes. The inkas are a very large tribe inhabiting the right bank opposite the Shilluks on the left and there is continual warfare between them. Schwenfarth says of them that they stand pre-eminent in the scale of the human race, their average height being five feet eleven inches. They must also be reckoned as one of the darkest races, although the deep black of their complexions gives place to brown when the ashes with which they rub themselves are washed off. They have a characteristic and peculiar posture. They stand on one leg with the other pressed against it almost at right angles. This stork-like attitude is very amusing when large numbers of them are seen together at the stopping places for the steamers.

The Dinkas employ a most ingenious system of cupping for many complaints. They use a cow's horn for the purpose. The skin is first wetted and then five cowhorns are applied at the large end, holes having been bored through the points. The doctor sucks these ends and plugs the holes one after another with cotton wool. After a time, the horns are removed and incisions made with a small knife. The process is then repeated. Finally the horns now filled with blood are removed and butter is rubbed on the skin.

Cupping is still extensively practised in Europe as well as in Africa, but strangely enough this valuable remedy is utterly neglected by British and American physicians. According to advanced medical theories, it is old-fashioned and therefore worthless.

The Shilluks are one of the largest tribes on the left bank of the river. They are very dark, of medium height and forbidding in appearance. Although very swarthy they belong to a less degraded class than most of the other natives in Central and Western Africa. Their huts are large and neatly kept. The dome-shaped roofs make them look like mushrooms.

One of the most easily recognized of all the African tribes is the Nyam-Nyams (Fuzzy-Wuzzeys). They are cannibals and look what they are, cruel and ferocious. They have the curious custom that it is unusual for them to take any meals in common except when dining on a member of a neighbouring tribe. Also the wife never eats with her husband except at the marriage ceremony, for it is a general rule that the women should never eat with the men. The King takes his meals in private. He must not be allowed to be seen eating and even the contents of his dish and anything left over from his plate are carefully thrown into a pit especially kept for the purpose.

They have a most objectionable form of salutation which is nevertheless considered a sign of the strongest affection, consisting of spitting on the face of a friend. The Nuer tribe also indulges in this custom and the traveller has to use the utmost tact to escape this unpleasant attention without offending their susceptibilities. Experience taught one to anticipate this token of goodwill by holding out the hand which then became the recipient of the salute. But among all the educated Shilluks, Dinkas and Nuers, the usual form of salutation is to hold out the outstretched hand, palm forwards, either above the head or above the level of the eyes.

The origin of the strange spitting salutation is unknown. Saliva was certainly used in the past as a cure for many diseases and also in the form of an amulet to ward off danger. It was believed to protect anyone from evil spells, especially when feasting, and from the dreaded evil eye, besides being used in various curious ways as a remedy for sorcery and a protection against serpents. Again, if you struck anyone and repented, all that you had to do was to spit on the hand used against the adversary and the pain would disappear. On the other hand, if you spat on your hand before striking him, the injury which you caused him would be aggravated.

The Azima or spitting cure has been an almost universal custom throughout the East from time immemorial. Those especially endowed with the power to effect this cure are the descendants of the Prophet and particularly holy men, though any human spittle is supposed to have curative properties. The operator usually kneels over the outstretched patient and after praying silently recites the Fatah aloud and then with pious ejaculations spits three times over the prone body, finally saying Amine (Amen). It may thus be conjectured that the Nile tribes mean well in their objectionable welcome to strangers who dislike it all the more because they are unaware of its inner significance.

The Dinkas, Shilluks and Nuers practise snake magic but it is difficult to discover many details about it as they are extremely reticent on the subject. The snake magician is considered a very wonderful and important personage and he is so astute that he seldom gives himself away. In order to practise snake magic, a cow or a goat must be kept to provide the snakes with a supply of milk, and these animals must not be given in exchange for wives or cattle. Other animals can also be used but the crocodile is considered the most potent. The magic itself largely consists of incantations, wearing charms, twisting and untwisting a small piece of string in a particular hut and leaving meat on the river bank for the crocodile.

It is very rare to meet an Arab in the Sudan who does not carry at least one talisman against the evil eye, another against evil spirits and one or two love charms. Those suspected of having the evil eye are shunned and avoided in every way. They are banished from one place after another, but the evil glance is believed never to take effect if a long white bone covered with soot is pointed at the person in question.

The belief in evil spirits is widespread among these tribes and according to them the world is peopled with a perfect army of genii, afreets, fairies and men changed into animals and vice versa. These evil influences have to be countered by innumerable charms, holy and mystic writings and quotations from the Koran, which forms a strange mixture of monotheistic religion and paganism. The casting out of devils is a very interesting performance and resembles in some respects the terrible Zaar in Cairo. It is performed by hereditary Fikis but sometimes by very clever old women. It is generally a long and tedious process in which charms, prayers, incantations, exhortations, cruelty and starvation all play a part. After the performance has lasted three or four days, the devil usually becomes restless and shows signs of wishing to depart from the possessed person who cries out: "Ana Marakat" (I am coming forth). If the Fiki is not present he is hurriedly summoned. On arrival he prays and asks the devil how he intends to come forth, to which the latter replies by the nose, mouth or eyes. The Fiki then calls upon him to come forth and laying his hands on his patient causes him such pain that he generally falls into a stupor, from which he wakes later in his right mind without any recollection whatsoever of the departure of his unwelcome guest or of what has been happening.

According to Major Gair Anderson, the Falatah who form such a considerable factor in the population of the large towns in the Province, have recourse to sand gazing for the purpose of making a diagnosis and predicting the course, treatment and issue of an illness. A small boy who has never been bitten by a dog or burnt by fire is used as a medium. He gazes on the word Allah scrawled on the sand and under the controlling eye of the Fiki calls upon the King of the Devils. By this time the child has sunk into a trance and he answers any questions put to him by the Fiki concerning the sick person. Sometimes water or a mirror are used instead of sand for the boy to gaze upon.

These performances of the Fikis seem to me highly instructive and suggestive. It is certainly a remarkable fact that only evil is invoked, as seems to be the case in most modern spiritualism. When we consider the unstable nervous and mental condition of these primitive people, the influence on them of suggestion, psychic concentration and animistic beliefs can be easily realized. Combined with a sincere faith in the powers of the supernatural, these influences must be potent factors in the cures which are undoubtedly accomplished.

I cannot leave the Sudan without referring again to the strange practices of circumcision which are still very general among both sexes. Boys are circumcised about the fifth or sixth year amid general festivity. Visitors from neighbouring villages attend and the operation is effectively performed by the local Hakim. Girls are circumcised at the same age but with less ceremony, while horribly cruel and barbarous mutilations are extensively practised.

The native women tattoo their lips and a more disgusting sight it is scarcely possible to imagine. In many parts of the Sudan, a very thick lip is considered attractive and a sign of beauty. In order to produce this unnatural hypertrophy, irritants are rubbed into the flesh and the operation is repeated several times. As far as I have been able to discover, the eyebrows are not interfered with among primitive people, the only instance being in ancient Egypt when they were shaved on the death of a cat. I have noticed that their semi-civilized sisters to-day do not wait for the death of a favourite pet to depilate or transform these few inoffensive hairs. I have seen scores of aged females who boast of having paid large sums of money to plastic surgeons for an operation to have their furrows removed. They would raise their wigs and proudly point to a long line, the tangible result of the operation. When I think of them I feel that the denizens of the great cities of the West are not so far removed from the native women in such tribes as the Dinkas, the Shilluks or even the Nyam Nyams as they would like us to imagine.

IX

AN American surgeon writing in a Medical Journal a few years ago said that if a modern embalmer were to proceed according to the methods used by the Ancient Egyptians, the only thing that would save him from being lynched would be his safe incarceration in a gaol by the health authorities.

There is certainly a big difference between the methods of embalming as practised in Ancient and Modern Egypt, and if the procedure and exorbitant fees sometimes demanded by the modern embalmer in the land of the Pharaohs to-day were known to my American colleague, there would be serious risk of international friction. But first of all, let us consider the history and origin of embalming. In the popular imagination, the custom of embalming the dead is almost exclusively associated with Ancient Egypt, but as a matter of fact other ancient peoples such as the Chinese, Tibetans, Incas, Guanches, Romans and Greeks also practised the art. Authorities on the subject believe that the custom was introduced by the Phœnicians and other traders who came from damper climates to the East. There is also biblical authority for associating the practice with the Israelites. Thus in Genesis we find that "Joseph commanded his servants, the physicians, to embalm his father and the physicians embalmed Israel." It is generally supposed that Joseph died at the age of a hundred and ten years. "They embalmed him and he was put in a coffin in Egypt."

In Ancient Egypt, the process of embalming seems to have had a deeply religious significance. Although the methods employed varied at different periods in the history of the country, as funereal beliefs developed the dead Osiris was looked upon as the prototype of dead men. Thus embalming was probably a preparation for the physical resurrection of the God Osiris. We find the following in an ancient manuscript: "Even as Osiris lives, he also will live; even as Osiris is not destroyed, he also will not be destroyed."

But when we come to think of the bliss which the souls of the blessed dead were supposed to enjoy in heaven with the gods, it is difficult to understand why these kings, queens, nobles and even poor people spent so much money to preserve the purely physical body from decay. Moreover, they arranged for a regular supply of sepulchral offerings which included not only food and drink but everything likely to make the dead comfortable and happy. The miscellaneous assortment of articles found in the tombs comprise household granaries and models, called Ushebiti, of labourers, servants, musicians and dancing girls. Amulets were also placed in the tombs to protect the deceased against snakes, scorpions and other animals.

Embalming was certainly considered of great religious significance. It was a sacred duty, the observance of which was essential to the spiritual welfare of the dead. The Ancient Egyptians thought that man consisted of a physical body, a shadow or double, a soul, a heart, a spirit called the Khu, a power, a name and a spiritual body. When the body died, the shadow departed from it and could only be brought back by the performance of a mystical ceremony. The double lived in the tomb with the body and was visited by the soul whose habitation was in heaven. The soul was a material thing like the Ka or double and was believed to partake of the funeral offerings. One of the objects of placing them in the tomb was to keep Khu there and to prevent it from wandering about in search of food. It may be stated with good reason that the immortal part of man that lived in the tomb was Ka, for a special part of the tomb, called the House of Ka, was reserved for it. The Ka or double was thus the ghost in the minds of the Egyptians in very early times. Later the Khu or Spirit became identified with it. There are frequent allusions in early manuscripts to the sanctity of the offerings made to the Ka.

They believed also that when a man or a woman died, the spirit or Ka went on living its life on earth with the same needs and pleasures as he or she had during ordinary life. It was a custom down to the pyramid age to place the utensils, weapons, tools and furniture used in life in the burial chamber of the tomb. The family either brought the offerings to the grave themselves or engaged persons by contract to carry out the service. This custom still persists in Egypt to-day. An Egyptian cemetery must therefore not be thought of as a city of the dead but as a city of the houses of the living spirits carrying on unseen the activities of the deceased while on earth. This is why the Egyptians spent so much money on the houses of their Kas. They wanted to protect the body from desecration or destruction and to provide the means for a happy and prosperous life in the world of spirits. According to one authority, the theory that the ghost possessed the form and characteristics of the person it tenanted led to the preservation of the dead body among the Egyptians in order to save the soul.

But in spite of all these theories and beliefs, no one can really say why the Egyptian embalmed his dead. It cannot have been entirely for the sake of preservation, as the soil of the country is so dry that bodies buried in it will be found well preserved after centuries. He believed, however, that he would return to earth and would inhabit his earthly shell, and in this I believe we find the fundamental reason for the preservation of the body by embalmment.

I do not pretend to understand, however, the relationship between the body, the soul, Ka and the Spirit. It is amazing that such an intelligent nation should have accepted such contradictory and meaningless practices and beliefs. But it is quite clear that in the treatment of the body, the chief aim was to preserve it and to enable it to retain its natural appearance, thus making it a fitting abode for the soul which they believed was immortal. But while no detail was overlooked in their attempt to preserve the body, it is also clear that the physical processes so carefully carried out were merely so many preparations for a higher spiritual existence. Indeed, as a certain writer points out, the Egyptians were so careful to show proper respect to everything appertaining to the human body that even the sawdust on the floor in the room where it was cleansed was neatly tied up in small linen bags and deposited in vases which were buried near the tomb.

But the most remarkable of all the sepulchral offerings

was undoubtedly the statue of the deceased which was placed in a small walled-in chamber near that of the offerings, with only a narrow slit in the wall between them. Thus the dead, if only in effigy, abided close to his worshippers and was in a position to profit from what was going on around him. It has even been suggested that perhaps it was thought his soul might quit his body in the mortuary chamber and inhabit this statue as a second body. But if this theory is correct, it is difficult to understand why they took the trouble of embalming the body in the first instance.

The inscriptions on the tombs themselves give us little help in solving the mystery. For example, what do we learn about the significance of such terms as Ka or spirit, the soul and the heart from the following sentences inscribed on tombs during the New Kingdom:

". . . that I may exercise myself upon the borders of my pool daily without ceasing, that my soul may hover on the boughs of trees which I planted, that I may cool myself under my sycamores, that I may eat the fruit which they give, that I may mount up to heaven and descend to earth and not be hindered on the way, that my Ka may not be waylaid, that my soul may not be shut up.

"Thou becomest a living soul: thou hast power over bread, water, air. Thou changest thyself into a phœnix, or a swallow, a sparrow hawk or a heron as thou desirest. Thou dost cross in the boat, thou sailest upon the water, thou livest anew and thy soul is not parted from thy body. My soul is a god together with the illuminated. Thou hast thine upright heart in thy possession and thy earlier heart belongs to thee. Thou possessed thy heart;

it doth not depart from thy body. Thy food is where it should be."

Even these few passages leave one completely bewildered. But it must not be forgotten that most of the information we possess has been obtained from the cemeteries of the dead. If anyone will take the trouble, as I have done, to visit cemeteries in many countries and examine epitaphs, he will nevertheless find ancient inscriptions that surpass in absurdity such passages as these. To write books on the manners and customs of the various peoples from such material would be manifestly absurd, and yet this is precisely what has been done by the Egyptologists. They laboriously attempt to decipher the most contradictory and extravagant allusions to a future state on a tomb and to draw conclusions about life in Ancient Egypt as a result. For instance, the so-called Book of the Dead which is considered of such importance in this respect is a compilation of texts from papyri or coffins in the tombs. There is no complete copy comprising all the chapters in existence. It largely consists of magical formulæ and allusions to mythical stories, a knowledge of which was essential to escape the perils and dangers of the future life. With all due respect to the Egyptologists, I think that many of the writers concerned must either have been humourists or else unscrupulous members of the priesthood who preyed on the fears and superstitions of ignorant people for their own material benefit. If they were treated humourously, no harm would be done; but when learned men write innumerable tomes in the mistaken attempt to elucidate a non-existent mystery, the matter ceases to be a joke and becomes ridiculous.

Let us leave them to their unprofitable studies and consider the process of mummification itself. This was obviously a most serious business in the minds of the people and played a most important part in their lives. When it originated amongst them is not precisely known, but according to Professor Elliot Smith the earliest evidence of mummification in Egypt consists of the mummy, said to be Ra Nefer, now in the Museum of the Royal College of Surgeons in London.

While examining remains in a series of Mastabas at Sakkara belonging to the second and third dynasties, Professor Elliot Smith found the skeleton of a woman completely invested in a large number of bandages that were still intact. Next to the body was a coarse cloth badly corroded, but the other layers of cloth were in a good state of preservation. The corrosion of the first cloth forms presumptive evidence that some substance, probably crude natron, had been applied to the body with a view to its preservation.

There have been and still are a number of lakes in Egypt which evaporate during the summer and leave crusts of various kinds of salt including Sodium Carbonate which in ancient times was used as a detergent. In the valley of Wadi Natrun, there are a number of these lakes yielding a crude salt called Natron which gives chemists their scientific name for sodium. It may be taken for granted embalmment existed in Egypt in the very earliest times and that natron or sodium was used for the purpose.

The finest examples of the art belong to the eighteenth and nineteenth dynasties, as shown by Sete I and Rameses II in the Cairo Museum. The latter especially is a remarkable specimen. The right arm is flexed and suggests a menacing attitude, as if that powerful monarch were justly indignant at the shameful indignities which he now has to suffer by being exhibited to the vulgar gaze of an irreverent crowd in a public museum. These indignities have certainly been inflicted by foreigners but the modern inhabitants of the country have not said a word in protest against them. I never gaze on the noble features of the great Rameses without feeling ashamed at the callous manner in which his remains have been treated. Recently a special mausoleum was erected for the mummies of the Pharaohs, but it has now been set aside for the body of the national hero, Zaghoul Pasha, and once more the desecrated bodies of the royal monarchs are to be relegated to the public museums.

In the earliest times, the process of embalming was effected by the injection of salt but later resin was used instead. It was an expensive matter and only those who were prepared to pay heavily for preservation could achieve it. When a person died, his body was first of all painted with red or yellow ochre and gum. Artificial eyes, usually onions, were inserted and the cheeks and neck were stuffed with clay. It was customary to remove the viscera and set it in four canopic jars, under the guardianship of four gods, until it was required later. It was removed by making a vertical insertion in the left flank. The thorax was not touched and very often, instead of replacing the viscera, the space was packed with bandages soaked in resin. The embalming wound was likewise stuffed with a resin-soaked plug.

A feature of embalming was the way in which the nails were tied. Each finger and each toe was treated separately, first being carefully tied with string and then bandaged to prevent the nails from dropping off. The operation was performed according to a definite order and ritual. Certain days were set aside for anointing the back with fat, and another period for gilding the body and so on. The process took thirty days in its entirety and bandaging a further forty. Burial usually took place on the seventy-first day from the beginning of the whole performance.

The most precise account of the methods of embalming among the Ancient Egyptians is to be found in Herodotus. He visited the country and has left the following account of the practice in use at the time.

"When in a family a man of any consideration dies, all the females of that family besmear their heads and faces with mud and then, leaving the body in the house, they wander about the city and beat themselves, having their clothes girt up and exposing their breasts. The men beat themselves likewise, being girt up in like manner. When they have done this, they carry the body out to be embalmed. There are persons appointed for this very purpose. When the body is brought to them, they show wooden models of corpses to the bearers. Having shown them all, they learn from the bearers in what way they wish the body to be prepared. Then, the relations, when they have agreed upon the price, depart; but the embalmers remaining in the workshops proceed to embalm the body in the most expensive manner. First they draw out the brains through the nostrils with an iron hook, taking part of them out in this manner, the rest by the infusion of drugs. Then with a sharp Ethiopian stone, they make an incision in the side and take out all the bowels, and having cleansed the abdomen and rinsed it with palm wine they next sprinkle it with powdered perfumes. Then having filled the belly with pure myrrh and cassia and other perfumes, they sew it up again; and when this is done, they steep it in natron, leaving it thus for seventy days. At the expiration of this time, they wash the corpse and wrap the whole body in bandages of flaxes cloth, smearing it with gum, which the Egyptians commonly use instead of glue. After this the relations, having taken the body back again, make a wooden case in the shape of a man and enclose the body in it. Thus having fastened it up, they store it in a sepulchral chamber, setting it upright against the wall. In this manner they prepare the bodies that are embalmed in the most expensive way."

Herodotus then goes on to describe the second and cheaper method.

"When they have charged their syringes with oil made from cedar, they fill the abdomen of the corpse without making any incision or taking out the bowels, but inject it at the fundament; and having prevented the injection from escaping, they steep the body in natron for the prescribed number of days, and on the last day they let out from the abdomen the oil of cedar which they had before injected, and it has such power that it brings away the intestines and vitals in a state of dissolution. The natron dissolves the flesh and nothing of the body remains but the skin and bones. When they have done this, they return the body without any further operation."

"The third method of embalming is this, which is used only for the poorest sort. Having thoroughly rinsed the abdomen in syrmæa, they steep it in natron for seventy days, and then deliver it to be carried away."

The Grecian historian Diodorus has also left a description which closely resembles that of Herodotus. He states: "The funerals of the Egyptians are conducted upon three different scales, the most expensive, the more moderate and the humblest. The first is said to cost a talent of silver (about £250 sterling); the second twenty-two minæ (or £60); and the third is extremely cheap. The persons who embalm the bodies are artists who have learnt this secret from their ancestors. They present an estimate of the funeral expenses to the friends of the deceased when they apply to them, and ask in what manner they wish it to be performed. This being agreed upon, they deliver the body to the proper persons appointed to that office. First one, who is called the scribe, marks upon the left side of the body as it lies on the ground the extent of the incision which is to be made. Then another who is called the dissector cuts open as much as the law permits, using an Ethiopian flint to cut the flesh. Then he immediately runs away pursued by those who are present, throwing stones at him amidst execrations, as if to cast upon him all the odium of this necessary act. For they look upon everyone who has offered violence to a human, or inflicted a wound or other injury upon him as hateful. On the other hand, the embalmers are held in the greatest esteem, being the associates of the priests and they are given free access to the temples as sacred persons.

"As soon as they have met together to embalm the body thus prepared for them, one introduces his hand through the aperture into the abdomen, and takes everything out, except the kidneys and the heart. Another cleanses each of the viscera with palm wine and aromatic substances. Lastly, after having applied oil of cedar to the whole body for upwards of thirty days, they add myrrh, cinnamon and those which have not only the power of preserving the body for a great length of time, but also of imparting to it a fragrant odour. It is then restored to the friends of the deceased. So perfectly are all the members preserved that even the hairs of the eyelids and eyebrows remain undisturbed and the whole appearance of the person is so unaltered that every feature may be recognized. The Egyptians, by keeping the bodies of their ancestors in magnificent apartments set aside for the purpose, are able to contemplate the faces of those who died many generations before them."

It is thus seen that the purely physical process of embalmment was very complicated and specialized, and also that it was carried out with great reverence and decorum. The same methods and prejudices concerning the treatment of a dead body are to be found in different parts of the world. Dissection was strictly forbidden and any attempt to do so was treated as a capital offence. It is interesting to note that in addition to the spiritual grace imparted to the body by the process of mummification, at a later period when the spiritual values had ceased to be recognized, the physical remains were utilized as medicinal agents with unqualified success. How mummy came to be used for medicinal purposes we do not know, but it was one of the drugs in ordinary use three or four hundred years ago and even much later. Neither can we say to what it owed its wonderful curative powers; probably we should be told to-day to radio activity or more likely to some new vitamine. But the fact remains that the demand for mummy was so great at one time that there was a shortage of the genuine article and bodies suffering from all sorts of diseases were treated with pitch to make them resemble mummies and then sold to purchasers. In 1564 Guy de Fontaine exposed these fraudulent devices and soon the Moslem authorities, on the look out for a new source of revenue, taxed out of existence what was a big business as well as a miraculous medicinal agent. It seems to have been used extensively for bruises, injuries and to stop hæmorrage. Francis I of France always had the powder mixed with rhubarb ready for use.

References to mummy in this respect are very common in literature. Shakespeare mentions it on many occasions. It is one of the ingredients of the witches' cauldron in "Macbeth". Falstaff in the "Merry Wives of Windsor" refers to it after his escape from drowning. Shirley's injunction "to make mummy of my flesh and sell it to the apothecaries" typifies the custom of the age. It even suggests that besides the ailments mentioned above for which it was used, it was also employed as a rejuvenator, thus forestalling the present vogue of glandular treatment. If it were so, there is no reason why pickled and spiced mummy should not be as efficacious as many of the so-called glandular treatments now flooding the market through enterprising manufacturing chemists. (In many instances, they are not only useless but definitely fraudulent; as rejuvenators, they are just about as much value as a pinch of mummy snuff.)

It is very degrading to think that human remains should be put to such purposes at times when people were supposed to be humane and civilized. But I am quite sure that if some enterprising charlatan advertised mummy powder to-morrow as an efficacious rejuvenator and beautifier, the remedy would immediately regain its popularity and achieve a wide sale.

Not so very long ago Conan Doyle exhibited in London what was known as the mysterious mummy hand. It was said to retain the spark of life, to be warm to the touch, to have belonged formerly to a royal princess and to have miraculous healing powers. Such is the credulity and gullibility of people that it caused considerable excitement.

The original owner of the hand, the veritable Princess, was said to have been discovered in Alexandria and through the usual spiritual channels to have made known that her hand went to England to find a certain person and that its warmth and frequent bleedings were her secrets. Having accomplished her mission of finding the person whom she sought, she apparently took no further interest in her hand, especially as it was being exploited from a mercenary point of view. For the sarcophagus of the Princess as well as her hand was supposed to bring good luck to all who touched it.

It is deplorable that the poor Egyptian should be subjected to such ignominious treatment after so much reverence, expense, ingenuity and skill had been expended to prevent his physical body from decay so that he and his Ka should enjoy everlasting peace in his tomb. All this digging, plundering, excavation and sacrilege is done in the interests of what is called science, but I doubt whether it has resulted in any further knowledge of great value or has advanced the happiness of mankind.

Tut-ank-Amen has been ignominiously despoiled of all

his treasures, which apparently he highly valued, but—
thanks to the energetic protests of Mr. Howard Carter—
he has been left in peace in his tomb. Mr. Harry Burton
and Mr. Lucas who were closely associated with the
operations in the tomb at the time of its discovery by
Mr. Carter, are in excellent health at the moment. This
statement can be made as positive evidence to refute the
absurd and sensational statements that are frequently
made concerning the mysterious deaths of persons connected with the tomb. Lord Carnarvon to be sure was
intimately associated with Mr. Howard Carter, but his
lamentable death, to my personal knowledge, can be
very easily explained on natural grounds.

The revival of the ancient myth concerning the traditional and mystical curse is due, I have authoritatively
been informed, to a certain journalist who was dis-
gruntled because special facilities were not offered to him
at the outset when there was an epidemic of collective
mental disturbance among newsmongers especially in
Luxor.

The whole trouble was due to the arrangement made
by Lord Carnarvon with *The Times* for the exclusive rights
of publication of details concerning the discoveries in
the Royal Tomb. It is difficult to see how any other
arrangement could have been made. If the representatives
of the local and foreign press had been allowed to loaf
about the Tomb waiting for news, the serious and delicate
operations associated with the cataloguing and preservation of the relics would have been seriously hampered.
But the monopoly created a great hullabaloo. The newspaper men and news agents at the time formed a cabal
and attempted also to induce the vernacular press to join

them, but to their credit their overtures met with only partial success. I remember very well one of the worst offenders publishing a violent tirade in one paper, but an intimation that the cowhide was in dangerous proximity acted beneficially, as shock therapy sometimes does.

Even Egyptologists joined in the campaign and it was not unusual to hear the discovery of Tut-ank-Amen's tomb alluded to as a spectacular exploit of great benefit to the proprietors of hotels but of little real scientific value. Mr. Howard Carter, as those who know him will readily admit, is a man of strong character. During his long residence in Egypt, he acted in accordance with the highest principles, even to the assertion of such principles to the detriment of his own interests.

At one period there was considerable friction between the French and English authorities in Egypt. Carter was then an Inspector of Antiquities in the service of the Egyptian Government. One day a party of French tourists visited some tombs of which he was in charge. Carter refused to admit them as he considered that they might do some damage to the ancient monuments as they were very drunk. They complained to the French Minister who in his turn complained to Lord Cromer. The latter sent for Carter and told him that he must apologize which he refused to do, preferring to resign from his position than to acknowledge that he had been in the wrong. His resignation revealed a man of strong character, for his salary was his only income at the time. It led him, however, to his remarkable work for Lord Carnarvon in the discovery and examination of Tut-ank-Amen's tomb.

Now let us turn to the modern side of the picture and

consider how the rite of embalming is carried out in Egypt at the present time. It is entirely confined to foreigners who have the misfortune to die in the country. It may be a family who set out expecting to have a pleasant and interesting trip, but suddenly one of the party is stricken with a fatal illness. All the arrangements have to be cancelled and the other members of the family return to their home, while the body of the deceased travels as a tragic cargo. Or it may be that a young person, the member of a large party, is left alone to die amongst total strangers as I have frequently known to happen. Amongst Jews and Mohammedans as well as local Christians burial takes place within twenty-four hours after death.

But in the case of foreigners who desire to be buried in their own country, as is almost always the case with Americans, certain procedures have to be carried out according to the regulations of the sanitary authorities whom it is wise to treat with due consideration, otherwise trivial technical difficulties may unexpectedly arise.

The methods employed now for the embalmment of the dead consist of the following:

A large artery, generally the carotid, is opened, a canula is inserted and a strong solution of formalin is allowed to flow slowly for twenty-four hours until two litres are used. An incision is then made. The viscera is removed and kept in a solution of formalin for twelve hours and then replaced in situ. The opening is then carefully closed, the body washed and covered with several layers of cotton wool and carefully bandaged, leaving only a portion of the face exposed.

Although it is a very gruesome undertaking, if it is

carried out with due reverence and proper feelings of sympathy and respect, nothing could be said against it considering the doctor's peculiar position and responsibilities. But when callousness, neglect of duty and financial extortion are involved, it assumes another aspect altogether, an aspect which reflects most discreditably on some members of the medical profession.

Extortionate fees have certainly been demanded for embalmment on many occasions. Owing to the scandal caused by these exorbitant prices, the English speaking doctors finally agreed several years ago that a maximum fee of one hundred Egyptian pounds should be charged for the process and this agreement was faithfully carried out for many years.

There is no doubt, however, that heartless extortion is regularly practised by many doctors. I have heard of three hundred and fifty pounds being asked from people of moderate means. Only a few years ago I was told of the case of a widow from whom a fee of two hundred and fifty pounds was demanded for the embalmment of her late husband. And to make matters worse, the process is often left to native temargiahs from whom it is foolish to expect the necessary skill or even proper respect for the dead.

"Embalming cases" are looked upon in modern Egypt (as doubtless they were in ancient times) as welcome sources of income. It has seriously depreciated of recent years, however, for the good reason that people can no longer afford to die in a foreign country. They must be content to die at home in their own beds. "Embalming cases" have thus ceased to provide the undertaker with his little joke. Not many years ago I met one of these gentlemen in the street. He was in great distress having recently lost a great friend of his, a medical man. But visibly brightening up, he asked me if there were any embalming cases in sight. On receiving a negative reply, he murmured gloomily: "What a miserable Christmas!"

X

A VISIT to Palestine is interesting enough at any time with the great and unique historic associations to be found in the country, but it is far more so now than at any other period in its history for it brings us at once into intimate contact with a serious and intricate international problem.

Palestine is the only land to be colonized since the new industrial revolution fully materialized. Although industrial unrest and unemployment have largely interfered with the scheme of colonization, the real difficulties which have been encountered are connected with persecution and the fear of persecution, racial pride, fanaticism and the natural desire of a large number of Jews to have a home and interest in the Holy Land. There is no doubt whatsoever that the persecutions in Germany have completely altered the original conception of a national home for the Jews in Palestine. This has further increased the difficulties and complications of a problem that was intricate enough in the first place.

Some time ago the Revisionist Zionist sent a petition to the League of Nations that ran as follows:

"Economic competition which has become intensified in all fields owing to the crisis, is swiftly forcing Jews out of all branches of economic life. . . . The unprecedented catastrophe of our German community which has shaken the very soul of World Jewry, has at the same time produced a further deterioration of the civil and material condition of the Jews far beyond the borders of the Third Reich. In a number of lands Jews are facing a situation of unmitigated despair without any prospect of improvement."

The conclusions drawn above are perfectly true, but it might also be said with equal truth that other nationalities and creeds see nothing but despair in the future. There is one big difference, however. Many of the Jewish refugees to be seen in Palestine and elsewhere formerly occupied good positions in the scientific world, but they have been compelled to abandon everything and are now to be found doing menial work in Palestine.

We hear a great deal about bird sanctuaries nowadays and as a bird lover I am in the fullest sympathy with everything that can be done to preserve them from destruction. But in our preoccupation with the safety of dumb creatures, there is a danger that the more serious question of human preservation is not receiving the consideration which it deserves. Palestine is to-day a human sanctuary, but unfortunately it is much too small for the overwhelming numbers of a persecuted race longing to find refuge there.

I have many good friends and patients among English and American Jews, and have reason to appreciate their excellent qualities and to rate them higher than those of some other nations. It was thus with considerable prejudice in their favour that I went to Palestine to examine the situation on the spot.

One of the first questions that interested me was that of immigration. In the beginning the Jews talked of tens of thousands of immigrants but they are now talking of hundreds of thousands. As the Government has definitely fixed the annual quota, Jews from all over the world have resorted to illicit immigration.

The Jewish agency justifies its demands by pointing to the shortage of labour. The absolutely Jewish city of Tel-Aviv had a population of 46,000 in 1931 but now it has risen to 100,000. The following is a letter which appeared in July, 1934, in the local English paper.

"Sir, Hordes of non-indigenous Arabs wander aimlessly about the streets of Jaffa and Tel-Aviv, earning a precarious living by cadging jobs as porters. I am told that a piastre will keep body and soul together for one day; a little dry bread and water suffices.

"These poor wretches have no homes. King George's Avenue is strewn with them day and night. A camp of dirty shacks on a waste piece of ground near by provides some sort of shelter for those who have been able to scrape together enough rags and sticks to form wigwams.

"The Jaffa Municipality has magnificent stables provided at a high cost, while near at hand, the S.P.C.A. possess an excellent hospital, all for animals; but these less fortunate of human form, through no fault of their own, have to fend for themselves.

"Down and outs have invaded Jaffa and Tel-Aviv in an almost vain hope of finding work, lured no doubt by supposed shortage of labour in the port. Is it not therefore incumbent upon the Jaffa Municipality to provide for such a contingency, unless some other body assists them, or a subvention is provided? The present situation is disgraceful."

When I was at Tel-Aviv, two hundred building projects were said to be held up because the contractors refused to accept the work for want of Jewish labour, as they would not employ Arabs.

It was the same in Haifa where an Englishman, a large employer of labour, told me that the Jews had been to him and threatened to leave his employ unless he discharged the Arabs and employed Jews instead, which he refused to do. He also told me (and he was in a position to know) that there was much unemployment in Haifa amongst both communities and that all the talk about shortage of labour was absolute nonsense.

The building trade was the busiest industry in the country, a bad sign in itself, but the large number of immigrants must have houses to live in, although these houses will neither provide food for their inhabitants nor for their builders.

Much unhealthy speculation was undoubtedly going on everywhere, especially in the neighbourhood of Tel-Aviv. Land was being sold at from one thousand five hundred to two thousand pounds an acre. Valuable orange groves were being cut down to make room for the new homes and workshops. The building trade was also very active at Haifa. The wealthier Jews have built their own homes there in their own plot of land and this partly accounts for the enormous amount of money coming into the country. But on the other hand, multitudes do not own houses and are now living on what amounts to a dole from the Jewish charitable organizations abroad. But this cannot go on for ever. Jews in other countries are not as wealthy as they once were.

When the dole ceases and the building trade slumps, their position will be even worse than before.

There is another side to this question of immigration and that is the rights of the Arabs, who after all have inhabited the country for over a thousand years. They have certainly allowed a great part of the land to go to waste through sheer neglect, and even to-day the land and villages of the Arabs can very easily be distinguished from those of the Jews; on the one hand, there are dirty squalid villages and badly cultivated lands, on the other, neat clean villages, well kept houses and the land cultivated on modern lines. But after allowing for all this, it must not be forgotten that Great Britain is trustee for the Arab as well as for the Jew, and if no limit is placed on immigration, the Arab will be completely swamped. The British have no right to permit this. In the Orange belt alone, the Arab is putting up a stern fight and appears to be holding his own, but how long will he continue to do so if he is left unprotected?

The question also arises whether the right kind of Jew is coming to the country as an immigrant. There appears to be a consensus of unbiased opinion that a very large proportion of undesirables are among them. This is largely due to the Revisionists who 'are bringing innumerable young men full of revolutionary ideas into the country. They are particularly active at Tel-Aviv and their activities have caused the city to have a very unsavoury reputation among the police. These young men are extremely arrogant and are the reason for much bitterness among the Moslem and Christian communities. It is quite a common occurrence for motorists to have to stop when they meet them in the street, as they refuse to make way with exaggerated insolence and impudence. Their defiant attitude is deeply resented and deplored by all friends of the Jewish National Home.

When we left Port Said, we had taken on board two hundred immigrants from a blue funnel steamer, I was told that these poor people had been detained at Aden for six weeks under quarantine regulations. They had originally come from Afghanistan. The man in charge of them told me that they belonged to the very ancient tribe of Gad and were the only survivors after innumerable massacres. Their complexions were copper coloured with dark hair curled up into ringlets in front of the ears. They seemed to be quiet, gentle people and when I saw them they were very thin and emaciated. One of the women had twins coming through the Canal but she had to board the ship at midnight. The following day I saw her go down the gangway at Jaffa with a baby under each arm. The policeman on duty sent her back, probably because the babies' passports were not in order.

And to think that these poor creatures, physical derelicts, had to travel such a long distance to escape persecution and to find a refuge in a human sanctuary! Truly man's inhumanity to man makes countless millions mourn!

In many of the Jewish settlements communistic principles are rigidly enforced. Like all such social experiments, they are attended by success in the beginning but only the future will show whether they are founded on a sound basis or not. Even now some of them do not present a very attractive appearance, especially such a settlement of Polish Jews, said to be very aggressive toward their Arab neighbours, situated on the Acre

Road outside Haifa. I visited one of these communistic settlements and if what I saw is typical of such people's ideas of morality, hygiene and the ordinary decencies of life, the outlook can only be described as disastrous. The conditions would be a disgrace to a Kaffir Krall. I certainly have not witnessed such utter degradation among primitive tribes in any part of the African Continent.

The Jews would be well advised to be more decorous in their dress and behaviour in public, if they are really in earnest in wishing the Arabs to co-operate with them in building their National Home. In any case, they must completely change their mental attitude towards them. The result of their present attitude is bound to be disaster. From what I heard, when three or four Arabs are talking together, the subject of their conversation is always the same. They are always threatening their heterogeneous neighbours.

The Jews undoubtedly feel that the immigration policy is biased against them at a time when their difficulties must command the sympathy of all humane persons.

The Arabs, on the other hand, feel that they are being swamped by a large number of immigrants, legal and illegal, and the serious Arab unrest is only kept under control by the authorities meting out equal justice to both parties.

Leaving the political aspect of the country, let me now mention some of the places of historic interest which I visited.

I do not believe that there is another district in the world where there has been as much strife and bloody warfare, so much treachery and so many murders, as in that which is situated between Acre and Mount Carmel.

Acre is mentioned for the first time in the Tablets of Tel Amarna. In 1291, it was beseiged by the Saracens from Egypt with 140,000 foot soldiers and 60,000 horsemen. After an heroic defence, it was captured and not a single person escaped the brutality of the conquerors. Even the nuns, who cut off their noses to escape a fate worse than death, were murdered. It was the last place held by the Crusaders. In 1799 Napoleon defeated the Turks near the city on the Kishon River. Mount Carmel and the River Kishon are associated with many stirring deeds of savagery. Even the prophet Elijah seemed to be affected by the brutality of the place, for we are told that the prophets of Baal to the number of four hundred and fifty were taken down to the River Kishon by Elijah —"and he slew them there."

This historic river even played its sinister part in the last war. A friend of mine who was then a Staff Officer has told me of the following tragic event which he witnessed on the spot. The General in command of the district sent a party of lancers along the beach near where the river enters the Mediterranean. Suddenly six of them were seen to be in distress. They began to submerge gradually, in spite of all the efforts of their comrades who made a circle round the spot. The poor fellows with their horses disappeared into the quicksands and the points of their lances were the last that was to be seen of these brave men who met this inglorious death. When Lord Allenby heard of the tragedy, he told the General with some annoyance that if he had read his Bible properly, he would not have sent his men where he did and the tragedy would have been avoided.

Lord Allenby's humanity and sense of humour are well illustrated by the following story. He was present at a garden party when a certain Minister Plenipotentiary of notorious vanity and self-importance appeared in the distance with his wife. On seeing them, Lord Allenby exclaimed in a sufficiently loud voice to be heard by those of us who were near him: "Look, look, see who is coming." Of course everyone turned round to the delight of the Minister who imagined that such marked attention was a compliment to his reputation.

While on the subject of diplomats, I cannot refrain from mentioning a very amusing incident that happened during the war. One day a friend of mine came to see me in great excitement to ask my advice as he believed that he had discovered a spy. He lived at Zeitoun outside Cairo, and every day a mysterious looking old gentleman with a black bag was in the habit of visiting a house not far from his own. I advised him to report the matter to the Commandant of Police and the Intelligence Department. He did so without obtaining the slightest satisfaction, so he decided to play the part of detective himself. He followed the mysterious looking old gentleman in his car and his suspicions were fully confirmed when it stopped in front of an historic building and a youthful, debonair and popular diplomat emerged from the motor car. Having met with such signal success, my friend determined to pursue his investigations which led him to make another important discovery: the other conspirator was no less than the wife of a well known personage in Cairo. When he told the Commandant of the result of his detective inquiry, the latter had to hold his fly whisk in front of his face to conceal his emotions.

But to return to the River Kishon. It is mentioned more than once in the Old Testament and mostly in a sinister manner. Obviously in very ancient days the river was much larger than it is now. In one place it is even alluded to as a mountain torrent. In Judges it is stated that "the River Kishon swept them away, that ancient river, the River Kishon." It obviously had an evil reputation even in those days.

The interesting point about the tragic incident of the lancers being swallowed up with their horses in quicksands is that it confirms certain statements in the Bible. I have alluded to it with some emphasis as it supports a theory of mine concerning certain fossil human bones recently excavated in Mount Carmel. I visited these excavations in 1934 and was kindly shown over one of the caves.

It appears that engineers in search of stone for the new breakwater at Haifa discovered a cave habitation of very ancient date. Subsequent investigation revealed a veritable cemetery and no less than ten skeletons embedded in a rock like stalagmite. Mr. Cowan of the University of California cut out great blocks of rock, some weighing more than a ton and each containing a skeleton, and had them transferred to the Royal College of Surgeons in London. He is now engaged on chiselling out the skulls and bones from the rock in which they have been embedded, according to Sir Arthur Keith, for thirty thousand years or perhaps twice that great period of time.

According to him also, they prove that for a very long period in prehistoric times, Palestine was inhabited like Europe by a race of Neanderthalians who like their European cousins shaped their tools in Monsterian manner. The strata above it contains stone tools of the Aurignacian culture and fossil bones of the modern type of man. Thus some twenty or thirty thousand years ago, the Neanderthalians of Palestine with their Monsterian culture must have been replaced by modern man and the Aurignacian culture. At first I was hopeful that they might prove to be the ancestors of modern humanity of which we are in search. These ancient cave men certainly have more of the modern man in their structural composition than have the Neanderthalians of Europe, but they nevertheless have the structural specialization which precludes the Neanderthalians from our ancestral line.

The question remains whether the Old Testament can help us to elucidate the mystery in any way. We read in Judges, "And the hand of Midian prevailed against Israel and because of the Midianites the children of Israel made them the dens which are in the mountains and caves and strongholds.

"And so it was, when Israel had sown that the Midianites came up, and the Amalekites and the Children of the East, even they came up against them."

They were beseiged for seven years in these caves and dens and strongholds and were greatly impoverished, as their enemies with all their cattle were encamped against them. They came as "grasshoppers for multitude" and laid bare the surrounding country as far as Gaza, so that great numbers of the Israelites must have died in the caves and were buried there.

It may be recalled that Elijah slew the prophets of Baal to the number of four hundred and fifty after he had compounded with them on the mountain, and the cave can be seen to-day where tradition says that he himself took refuge. The whole mountain is full of caves and dens especially on the sea shore, where the Israelites at various periods sought refuge from successive persecutions. In the First Book of Kings we read: "And he said go forth and stand upon the Mount before the Lord. And behold, the Lord passed by and a great and strong wind rent the mountains and broke in pieces rocks before the Lord; but the Lord was not in the wind, and after the wind an earthquake, but the Lord was not in the earthquake. And after the earthquake a fire, but the Lord was not in the fire and after the fire a still small voice."

This obviously refers to a volcanic eruption as well as to an earthquake. The grand Rabbi of Cairo, a noted scholar, has informed me that it is the only earthquake mentioned in the Old Testament, but said that there were undoubtedly many others in ancient times. In our own era, we have a record of one in 1202 which devastated Acre and the surrounding country.

I was so impressed by the geological formation of the district that I made inquiries as to whether there was any history of serious earthquakes. On receiving a negative reply, I determined to inquire further into the matter with this result. The fact that a very serious earthquake accompanied by a volcanic eruption had possibly occurred in the district may account for the fossil skulls and other human bones being embedded in the rock matrix. But let it be noted, Sir Arthur Keith said, that the remains were embedded in a "rock like stalagmite." Now as stalagmites are formed from below by lime deposited on the floors of caverns by water dropping from the roof, to an ordinary observer like myself who knows little about Monsterian deposits or tools, an explanation of the fossil remains in the rock matrix immediately offers itself, especially when we know that these caves were veritable cemeteries for centuries.

In my very interesting interview with the Grand Rabbi of Cairo, he informed me that in prehistoric times Palestine was inhabited by giants who lived in caves in the mountains, and that in later times during the Maccabean revolution in 250 B.C. (Jewish calendar), the people took refuge in the caves of Mount Carmel and were buried there.

Moreover, in 180 B.C., the Jewish ecclesiastical tribunal ordered that all bodies should be buried near rivers (previously the dead had been buried in their own gardens) and left undisturbed for one or two years, after which the bones were to be given to the relations to be buried as they desired. If the remains were not claimed by the friends, then they were buried in the caves in the mountains.

Moreover, during the reign of Hadrian 132 B.C., when the Israelites rose against the Romans, they also took refuge in the caves, especially those along the sea shore, and were buried there. All this proves that in the caves and dens of Mount Carmel fossil remains of every description should be found.

It is now for the reader to draw his own conclusions. In any case there is no harm in adding one more hypothetical link to the long chain of conjectures associated with the early history of mankind.

XI

A GREAT deal has been written about Ancient Medicine, most of it pure nonsense, but very little of any value of the art of medicine as practised among the Ancient Egyptians.

My attention was arrested by the frequent allusions of orators delivering their orations before learned societies to "the wonderful knowledge and skill displayed by the ancient practitioners unsurpassed to-day" and I thought the subject well worth serious study. It seemed all the more so when I heard some of the remarks of these florid speakers, such as: "As we advance in our knowledge of the Ancients, we find that we are poor imitators, and that in Egypt, thirty-five thousand years before Christ, the doctors had very much the same knowledge as we have ourselves". I remember another speaker saying with the utmost assurance: "One is really obliged to ask oneself whether the world has progressed from the days of Sesostris to those of Pasteur, or if humanity does not go back a pace in one direction when it advances in another".

Before proceeding in my studies, I called on the late Sir Gaston Maspero, who was then at the head of the Antiquities Department in Egypt. He received me most affably and gave me every facility, even lending me some unpublished manuscripts written on the subject by himself. I was very astonished when at the very outset he told me with a genial and significant smile: "The Ancient Egyptians knew little or nothing about medicine. What they knew is not worth knowing". Such an emphatic opinion, emanating from one of the greatest Egyptologists, who had made an exhaustive study of all the important medical works surviving from Ancient Egypt, was impressive and convincing and should be accepted as authoritative.

The most important of these ancient medical works are the Ebers Papyrus in Leipzig, the Berlin medical Papyrus now in that city, the Hearst Papyrus in the University of California and the Edwin Smith Papyrus now the property of the New York Historical Society.

The value of these documents from the medical point of view is considerably limited by the fact that out of the eight hundred and eleven recipes in the Ebers Papyrus, only forty-seven are accompanied by a diagnosis of the malady treated, while the Hearst and Berlin Papyri have even fewer, that is to say one and two respectively.

The Ebers Papyrus coming from Thebes and therefore representing the great Theban School or priesthood, bears the mark of riper knowledge and perhaps more systematic arrangement, but the first three contain much in common and originating as they evidently do from the same source or sources, equally reflect the thought and practice of the day.

Every ache and pain was supposed to be subject to supernatural influences and disease was held to be caused by the entrance into the body of demoniacal or evil spirits who produced pathological changes in proportion to their malignity or power for evil. No serious attempt was made to define a disease or to describe it as a separate morbid entity. Needless to say they had not the slightest knowledge of specific or infectious maladies, while contagion was not even mentioned or suspected. They frequently confounded under the same name entirely different maladies. For the most part, the Egyptian name does not mean the same thing as the modern and thus the value to be placed on the interpretations of the documents remains doubtful.

There are some curious diagnostic aphorisms in the Ebers Papyrus. One concerns what is called cancer It seems probable that malignant disease was extremely prevalent in ancient times. The other diagnosis concerns an affection of the Rohet which presumably means the stomach, where the importance of certain symptoms are clearly recognized. The aphorisms mostly relate to the abdomen and affections of the chest, heart and blood vessels, but it is difficult to find out exactly what is meant by such terms as the Hati, the Meres and the Rohet.

But taking everything into consideration, the Ebers Papyrus is the most reliable and must be accepted as the standard work. It certainly conveys a better impression of their very meagre medical knowledge and its practical application than any other document known to us.

There is one very interesting passage concerning the circulation, the importance of which has been tremendously exaggerated. Some people even go so far as to maintain that the Ancient Egyptians knew all about the circulation of the blood long before Harvey's discovery. An identical passage, although not so exhaustive, appears in the Edwin Smith Papyrus which suggests a common origin. In this passage, the physician is asked to put his fingers on the head, hands, arms and legs of the patient and feel the motions of the heart as they come through the vessels permeating these members. Again, it is pointed out that if a suppurative disease forms in the body, the result is that abcesses form in various parts from the heart causing the septic matter to pass through the blood vessels, which produces fever and inflammation of various kinds in the body. This is one of the most important observations made in any of the medical documents. The heart was probably thought of as a pump, but there is nothing to indicate that they had the faintest idea of its structure. They seem to have failed to distinguish between the veins and the arteries as they are referred to indiscriminately by the same term. The heart apparently was considered as an active, propelling force which conveyed the necessary requirements through canals to all parts of the body, including the effect of disease as well as remedies for such disease.

From the enumeration of these canals in the Ebers Papyrus, it is clear that they considered these vessels as supplying the organs indicated, some with blood, some with water and some with air. For instance, we find such a passage as—"As for the air that enters the nose, it enters to the heart and lungs and they convey it to the whole body." But there is nothing to indicate that they were aware of a return flow to the heart. They certainly had not even the most rudimentary knowledge or suspicion of the vital chemical changes which are taking place all the time, even in what they called the canals. There is no certainty about the exact meaning of the term, Mt-W, which they used for them. From their frequent mention of it, it quite probably meant the nerves, ligaments and muscles besides the veins and arteries. In any case, they were all considered vital to health. In the inscriptions on the tombs, the wish for a person's good health is often found expressed thus—"may his Mt-W flourish, be comfortable or be excellent".

In the Hearst Papyrus, the prescriptions simply refer to the parts of the body affected. There are remedies for such injuries as fractured bones and the bites of crocodiles, pigs, lions and men, although curiously enough dogs are not mentioned in this respect. Human nature would appear always to have been the same, for there are prescriptions for blood purifiers, hair restorers, dyes, cosmetics, pain killers, soothing syrups (containing opium), beautifiers and of course love filters in great number and variety. There are two hundred and sixty-nine prescriptions in all but only one diagnosis or attempt at diagnosis. It ends with the words—"It is concluded with peace"—but whether for the unfortunate patients can only be conjectured.

The Berlin Papyrus differs in no essential particular from the Hearst. There are several prescriptions of the usual nature, numerous incantations and only two attempts at diagnosis.

From the anatomical point of view, the views of the Ancient Egyptians seem to have been even more fantastic than might be expected from the fact that the dissection of the human body was only allowed for a short time in Alexandria in about 300 B.C. The earliest anatomists taught that a certain number of vessels went to each part of the body, four to the nostrils, two to the blood, four to the interior of the temples and four to the ears. They believed that "the breath of life enters by the right ear and the breath of death by the left". At a much later period some progress was made but nothing is more striking than the non-progressive character of Ancient Egyptian medicine. From the time of King Menes of the first dynasty and the first historical personage to be associated with medical art, to that of the Ptolemies, not a single advance was registered either in theory or practice. This is a remarkable fact and no satisfactory explanation has ever been forthcoming. In their fulsome adulation of the Ancients, the scientists of the twentieth century seem to have forgotten their views concerning evolution.

Magic and not anything that can possibly be termed science in any form was the foundation of Ancient Medicine. The Egyptians in those early days believed that magic gave them complete powers over Nature, including of course disease and its supposed demoniacal origin. For thousands of years in Egypt and elsewhere, the magician exercised complete power over everything and was thought to represent the highest state of intelligence. The earliest healing art was psychological. The supreme power of the magician is reflected in the three papyri which I have mentioned. Both he and his incantations never lost their authority up to the beginning of the present era, and they are very far from having lost it even to-day.

I have already mentioned the opinion of Sir Gaston Maspero, let me quote some opinions of another great authority on the subject, Professor Breasted. Referring to the three principal papyri, the standard works of the Ancient Egyptians, he says:

"So-called translations of the Ebers Papyrus have been made, with misunderstandings on every page which make them look ludicrous and much popular writing based on such translation has professed to give us some account of Egyptian Medicine. Such discussion is of course, not only without value, but very misleading.

"All of the three papyri are merely haphazard collections of recipes mingled in an indescribably confused hodge-podge. All these treatises were the working tools of superstitious practitioners of demoniacal medicine.

"To sum up this comparison then, the other leading medical documents of Ancient Egypt are each a hodge-podge of miscellaneous recipes dominated by magic from beginning to end, while the old Book of Surgery and External Medicine appears by contrast as a unique organization of cases containing, especially in diagnoses, more scientific medical discussions than all the other surviving Ancient Egyptian Medical documents combined."

This condemnation of the accepted authoritative medical works of Ancient Egypt is very emphatic and has not received the attention which it deserves. But it must be remembered that he was contrasting the comparative merits of the three papyri and was equally emphatic concerning the great scientific value of the Edwin Smith Papyrus which he translated himself. He even goes so far as to say that the Edwin Smith Roll offers us enough information to enable us for the first time to form a reliable estimate of the character and importance of Egyptian medical knowledge.

Professor Breasted's translation of the Edwin Smith Papyrus is a monumental work and it is certainly not his fault if "Our Surgeon", as he calls its Egyptian author, has not earned for himself an enduring place as the first scientific surgeon, but I doubt whether any surgeon would be very impressed by his achievements from a study of the manuscript which I personally consider of no scientific value whatsoever.

In his enthusiasm, the Professor seems to consider the claims of the great and immortal Hippocrates as secondary to "our scientific surgeon" and makes the remarkable statement that "the Hippocrates school was far more interested in the human body when it was sick than when it was well, and furthermore was evidently more inspired by a desire for knowledge than by the hope of curing the patient", opinions to which no educated medical man would subscribe.

It is obvious that there must be some substantial grounds for such extravagant claims especially when made by such a renowned Egyptologist as Professor Breasted, and they thus seem worthy of closer examination.

The forty-eight cases in the treatise (all injuries except two) begin at the top of the head and proceed downwards to the spine where the document breaks off. The arrangements are very systematic and methodical, even to the extent of the cases gradually increasing in severity. The discussion of each case comes under the following headings: Title, Examination, Diagnosis, Treatment and an explanation of the obscure terms employed in the description of the cases. Here is an example of the usual procedure.

Title "Instructions concerning a gaping wound in the head penetrating to the bone and splitting the skull."

Examination "If thou examinest a man having a gaping
wound and thou shouldst place thy hand on him,
or thou shouldst probe, or inspect or examine the
wound and thou shouldst find . . .

Diagnosis Thou shouldst say concerning him—one
having . . . followed by a description of what is
actually seen in the wound, as well as symptoms,
if any, present.

Verdict and Treatment
  1. An Ailment which I will treat.
  2. An Ailment with which I will contend.
  3. An Ailment not to be treated.

It is somewhat remarkable that out of the forty-eight
cases mentioned, fourteen were considered hopeless and
received no treatment, and these were nearly all compound fractures or supposed to be so. For instance, under
the heading of ailments not to be treated we find, "Dis-
location of two collar bones having a rupture of the
tissue over it, penetrating to the interior," and "one
having a break in the upper arm over which a wound has
been inflicted, piercing through."

As regards the diagnosis, swelling beneath the scalp
was frequently accepted as a sign of a depressed fracture
because there was a ring of fibrinous matter round the
injury.

But this is not the place in which to enter into questions
of diagnosis but rather into the interpretation of certain
signs and symptoms and the treatment suggested for
them. According to Professor Breasted, the word
"brain" or some word signifying the existence of such
an organ was first used in this surgical treatise. But their

idea of the anatomy of the brain may be gathered from their comparison of the convolutions with "the corrugations which form on molton copper". A puncture of the skull is likened to "a broken hole in a pottery jar". Furthermore, they speak of "the membrane or skin enveloping the brain being rent so that it breaks open the fluid in the interior of the head".

They noticed the fact that injuries of the head involving the brain affected the movements of the upper and lower limbs, as well as the eyes, facial appearance, the powers of speech and the hearing. But they state that the paralysis and other symptoms occurred on the same side of the body as the injury to the head which we now know to be entirely wrong. In any case, the suggestion that "the ancient surgeon" had the remotest idea of the functions of the brain because of this observation cannot be entertained for one moment.

Their observations with regard to anatomical appearances were crude but exact. Likewise they describe quite accurately certain symptoms, but this is not very surprising when certain facts are considered. For instance, fractured bones have been found in three out of every hundred skeletons that have been exhumed. Compound fractures and dislocated joints must have been extremely common among the two hundred thousand men working for twenty years on the construction of the Great Pyramid. Considering how frequently fractures must have occurred, it is not surprising that they were very skilfully treated. But you see such operations carried out with quite as much skill by the witch doctors and ju-ju men among savage tribes in Africa to-day, and their experience of such injuries is comparatively limited compared to their Egyptian colleagues thousands of years ago.

Professor Breasted has expended much scholarly care on establishing the point that the Egyptian surgeon fully realized the importance of noting the pulse in cases of injury. As we have seen from the extract from the Ebers Papyrus, they were aware that if the fingers are placed on certain specified parts of the body, the action of the heart can be measured because of its pulsation in every vessel of every member. Although these passages are obscure, they suggest that they believed the progress of injuries or wounds was reflected on the heart and blood vessels with the result that this progress could be estimated according to the rate of the pulse. The gravity of septic conditions causing fever was realized and when they occurred, the injunction not to bind or bandage was rightly enjoined.

I fully appreciate the systematic manner in which the cases were arranged by the "Surgeon", and also his skill in describing the various kinds of fractures with his limited vocabulary, mentioning the symptoms peculiar to each. But there are many serious omissions and errors through ignorance which greatly detract from the scientific value of the papyri as a surgical document.

On the other hand, the Ancient Egyptian Surgeon cannot be too highly praised for the high ethical standard which he displays in many of his cases. Whatever one may think of his merits as a practitioner, one cannot but admire his sterling rectitude which is apparent on every page of the document. It is clear that he would not approve of many modern methods. Few doctors would now refuse to treat an ailment on ethical grounds but their interest in their patients does not continue after death as his obviously did, considering his chapter on embalming.

The main weaknesses of this ancient surgical treatise may be classified thus:

(1) The lack of any knowledge of hygiene and sepsis. No mention is made whatsoever of cleanliness. The word is not used in any sense.

(2) The condition of the tongue (which at least is as important as the pulse) is never mentioned.

(3) Trepanning, the only rational treatment in many cases was not resorted to, because it was unknown. This one fact in itself betrays gross and inexcusable ignorance on the part of the surgeons of the period, especially since we know that the operation was performed by ancient peoples in other countries and also considering the enormous number of head injuries for which it was clearly indicated. Instead, the routine treatment consisted of fresh meat for one day followed by grease and honey. Considering that the meat was doubtless stale and contaminated by flies, it was truly barbaric treatment. As for tetanus, the only recommendation was that the stiffness in the neck should be rubbed with grease.

(4) There is no indication as to the number of the recoveries.

These are very serious defects. And yet so great is the popular adulation of this "Ancient Surgeon" that at the annual oration before the Medical Society of London in 1934, Professor Gask said, "that the modern surgeon should raise his hat to the Ancient Egyptians for their cleanly and rational method of treatment." He forgot to mention that ox dung was frequently used for poultices or dressings (it is mentioned twice in the Edwin Smith Papyrus) and that human brains were used for the same purpose in eye diseases.

But the fact of the matter is that, as the late P. J. Barnum rightly said, the public loves to be humbugged and the subject of Ancient Medicine is no exception to the general rule. Even Lincoln with his proverbial goodwill towards mankind admitted that "you can fool part of the public all the time and all the public part of the time."

But before leaving this interesting surgical treatise to be exploited by its admirers, I must mention one very curious expression which occurs nine times amongst the directors for treatment. It consists of the words—"Moor him to his mooring stakes", or as it has been variously translated: "Put him on his fingers" and "Put him on his accustomed diet without giving him any prescription". It is impossible not to admire the correct attitude of this ancient practitioner, but he must also have been a pedant playing the part of a humourist, a type not unfamiliar to medical students. In the treatment of disease and injuries, diet was considered of considerable importance by the ancient doctors and surgeons, but I doubt whether the modern surgeon would agree that the patient should be "moored to his mooring mast" when suffering from many of the injuries mentioned in the Edwin Smith Papyrus.

Now let us consider the diet as ordinarily prescribed in sickness by the ancients. Fruit and vegetables played a large part in it. According to Herodotus, the diet of the men who built the Pyramids consisted of Taphanus (now called Rigl) or onions and garlic, but he omitted to mention lentils which have always been used extensively in Egypt.

Melons, leeks, and cucumbers were largely eaten and cabbages were consumed with the express purpose of exciting a desire for alcoholic drinks, although considering the climate of Egypt they seem quite unnecessary.

In the houses of the rich, bread was made from wheat but among the poorer classes, cakes of barley were substituted.

The priests were most particular about the quality of their food. Beans were held in utter abhorrence, while lentils, peas, garlic, leeks and onions were strictly forbidden although all these vegetables were placed as offerings on the altars of the Gods.

Quite apart from the influence of demoniacal possession, it was recognized that disease could be caused by irregularities or excess in eating. For this reason, abstinence was enjoined. Emetics and laxatives were also employed for relieving the system. It is asserted that for three days every month a regular course of treatment was pursued. But notwithstanding such wise injunctions, irregularities and excesses and even regular orgies of eating and drinking were by no means uncommon, as can be seen by representations of drunken ladies being helped to their homes by their servants on the walls of the temples. From accounts of the annual festival at Bubastis, sufficient material could be gleaned by one of our sensational novelists for scenes of unparalleled obscenity, licentiousness and vulgarity.

As every ache and pain was supposed to be subject to

supernatural influences, both as to cause and cure, every remedy was prepared with prescribed incantations of words. There were certain charms to be spoken when using a bandage. While the evil effects of magic could be dispelled by a compound of soda, dates, hair fruit and incense, well mixed and swallowed with beer.

The physicians, as the responsible interpreters of a supernatural science, made great reputations for themselves in the treatment of functional or minor ailments by the judicious mixture of a few grains of divinity with ingredients of a more terrestrial origin. To be efficacious, all remedies were accompanied by a magical formula varying according to the disease in question. For instance when treating anything the matter with the eye, the incantation always terminated with an adjuration to the crocodile.

The actual remedies employed consisted of such things as honey, castor and olive oil, linseed, opium, juniper, nepenthe (probably hashish), colchicum, absinth, vinegar, sodium, iron, antimony, magnesia and mercury. They were made up into potions or injections and frequently mixed with water, oil, beer (largely used), barley water, wine, milk and honey. For the pills and ointments, bulky ingredients such as animal fat, oil or wax were added.

Although truth compels me to say that the time-honoured physicians of Ancient Egypt were not in fact the wise and profoundly learned men of medicine that they have been represented to be, and that much which they taught was fallacious in principle and absurd in practice, I give them unstinted praise for appreciating the value of plain and simple living.

No reference to Ancient Medicine would be complete without allusion to the mysterious wise man and Egyptian God of Medicine, Imhotep.

At the International Congress on Tropical Medicine in Cairo in December, 1929, I read a paper on Imhotep but shortly before reading it I heard that a special medal with the figure of the God inscribed on it was being distributed to the members of the Congress in commemoration of the event. As my paper was not exactly complimentary to the Wise Man, I felt it only right to omit some of the more critical passages. In July, 1933, however, I fully elaborated my views concerning Imhotep before the History of Medicine Section of the British Medical Association in Dublin.

I have attempted to prove, and according to such a great authority as Mr. Howard Carter I have succeeded in doing so, that not a shred of trustworthy evidence has been produced to show that Imhotep was a medical practitioner, and that his deification was due to his powers as a magician.

Let me first of all examine the contrary views. Sir William Osler said "he was the first physician to stand out clearly from the mists of antiquity" and the late Dr. Hurry alluded to him in an exhaustive work as "a fine type of scholarly physician", comparing him to Aristotle. Professor Breasted conjectures that he may very well have written the Edwin Smith Papyrus, apparently conveniently forgetting that it is a purely surgical treatise.

Now Imhotep has always been associated with the cure of insomnia, barrenness, the interpretation of dreams and incubation sleep, proving that his fame partly rested on his great magical powers and wisdom and even more on the myths and legends which, when constructed with skill as they were by the Ptolemies two thousand years after his death, could be made to serve diverse ends and even suggest that he had profound esoteric knowledge.

For thousands of years, as Herodotus has recorded, Thoth was considered the God of Medicine by the Egyptians and honoured as such.

Imhotep was the son of Ptah and formed one of the Memphite triad. He was looked upon as a God and as such only had a mythical existence until his name was resuscitated by Sethe and the German school and a purely human origin was ascribed to him, although the name of his alleged mother, Krednoukh, only appears late in Egyptian history.

What Sethe and other Egyptologists consider of prime importance in proving the human origin of Imhotep was found in a quarry in the neighbourhood of the Red Sea. It appears that an obscure architect in the distant past amused himself in his spare time by recording the fact that he was the direct descendant of Imhotep, mentioning twenty-five ancestors, all architects, to prove his statement. Now how many people even in modern times could state precisely the names and occupations of twenty-five of their direct ancestors? Such evidence carries no weight. It is the earliest example of a faked pedigree. There is not a shred of evidence to show that Imhotep was the first Physician of Antiquity. Several well known names of the early dynasties, including Kings such as Menes and Zoser were undeniably associated with the art of medicine. Some of them are mentioned in the papyri as having written books on medicine but the name of Imhotep does not appear anywhere. Until Sethe dethroned him, Seckhemet, whose stele is in the Cairo Museum, was considered the first physician.

Dr. Pepi Ank was also a versatile practitioner. He tells us that he was the doctor of the King's belly as well as the administrator of Clysters, the intimate and occulist of Pharaoh and the man who prepared the *hein*, an unknown remedy.

Even among the famous magicians of the period, the name of Imhotep is conspicious by its absence. This is more than a coincidence when considered in connection with the following incident. The Herutataf who is mentioned was prominently associated with Imhotep in the famous drinking song, "The Song of Harper", to be heard in the beer shops all over Egypt.

In the Westcar Papyrus a wonderful feat is mentioned. It appears that Herutataf, the son of Cheops, who was famous as a learned man and whose name is mentioned in the Book of the Dead, told his father that he knew of a sage called Teta who was one hundred and ten years old and yet ate five hundred loaves of bread and the shoulder of an ox and drank one hundred measures of ale. "He knoweth how to fasten a head that has been cut off on to its body, he knoweth how to make a lien follow him while his snare is trailing on the ground". Herutataf brought Teta into the presence of his father and he successively decapitated a goose, another bird and an ox. The heads and bodies were then placed at a considerable distance from each other. Teta murmured some magic words and the parts moved towards one another and resumed their natural positions.

Another remarkable incident is mentioned in the same

papyrus. It happened when Imhotep is alleged to have flourished but again his name is not mentioned. It is very significant that Teta and Abu-aner, the protagonists in the story, were chief Lector Priests like Imhotep.

It is recorded that Prince Khaf-Ra told Cheops a story of an event that happened in the time of Neb-Ra, a King of the Third Dynasty, about 3830 B.C. It seems that this king paid a visit to one of the high officials called Abu-aner, whose wife fell violently in love with one of the soldiers in the royal suite. The lady sent a message to her lover and they agreed to meet at a certain house. The steward who prepared the house for them went to his master, Abu-aner, and told him everything. Abu-aner ordered him to bring him a box out of which he took a quantity of wax. Then he made a model of a crocodile and recited certain magical words over it, adding: "When the man cometh down to bathe in my waters, seize him." Turning to the steward, he gave him the crocodile and said: "When the man according to his daily wont cometh down to wash in the water, thou shalt cast the crocodile into the water after him." On the following day, the wife of Abu-aner ordered the steward to make ready the house again and when the man went down to bathe as usual, the steward went also and threw into the water the wax crocodile which immediately became a living crocodile twelve feet in length that seized its prey and dragged him into the water. Meanwhile, Abu-aner remained with his King for seven days and throughout that time the victim remained in the depths of the water. On the following day Abu-aner went out with the King for a walk and invited His Majesty to come and see for himself a wonderful thing which had happened to a man in his own days. The King went with him and when they came to the water, Abu-aner addressed the crocodile, saying: "Bring hither the man," whereupon the crocodile appeared with the man. The King remarked: "What a horrid looking monster!" Abu-aner stooped down and took it in his hand and it straight away became a waxen crocodile again. Then Abu-aner told the King what had happened between his wife and the man whom the crocodile had brought out of the water, whereupon the King said to the crocodile: "Take that which is thine and begone." It immediately seized its victim again and disappeared into the depths. By the royal command, the erring wife was seized and led to the north side of the palace and burnt and her ashes cast into the stream.

And in the whole of this story there is no mention of Imhotep!

The omission of any reference to him among his colleagues, medical and magical, alleged to be his contemporaries is in itself very remarkable and requires a good deal of explanation. But there is still more convincing evidence of a negative character in the absence of any allusion to him in the ancient monuments or in the medical papyri. His name does not even appear in the Book of the Dead, neither is he mentioned by any of the contemporary sages, such as Hardadef, Kegeni or Ptahotip, many of whose wise sayings survive and would well repay perusal. Even later writers such as Herodotus, Hippocrates, Diodorus or Clemens make no mention of him, although the two former visited Egypt not long after the period when he was deified. It is left to Manetto alone to do so, and he said that Imhotep and Zoser were Identical. Unfortunately little or nothing is known about Zoser, the builder of the step Pyramid. The only contemporary evidence about Imhotep appears on a royal statue recently discovered in Sakkara by Firth, deciphered by Gunn and now in the Cairo Museum.

The inscription on the statue runs: "The Chancellor of the King of Lower Egypt, Chief under the King of Upper Egypt, Administrator of the Great Mansion, Hereditory Noble, Heliopolitan High Priest, Imhotep."

He thus appears here as a simple functionary of the King. With the exception of the rank as High Priest, none of the titles are in any way exalted and certainly not those usually assigned to the traditional Vizier by his admirers.

The omission of all reference to the Medical Art proves conclusively that he was not recognized in those early days as a Physician; it remained for the Ptolemies two thousand years after his death to discover that important omission. But they made up for the neglect by deifying him and associating him with their God Asklepios without recording a single valid reason. But all these honours were doubtless bestowed on him for good religious and political reasons. It should be noted also that deification was not effected by his own countrymen but by foreigners settled in Egypt.

At one time the late Mr. Firth, who until a few years ago was in charge of the excavations at Sakkara, was convinced that he was on the point of discovering Imhotep's tomb but later found that he was mistaken and entirely agreed with my views concerning the "Wise Man".

This absence of all contemporary evidence, apart from the statue just mentioned, provides serious objections to the acceptance, as established facts of scientific value, of a series of biographical incidents mentioned by foreigners two thousand years after his death and based largely if not entirely on myths and legends.

Imhotep means "He who comes in Peace". Probably the great desire of his Ka would be to be left in peace and saved from the picturesque and exaggerated eulogies of certain Egyptologists, visionaries and medical orators who confuse fairy tales with the true facts.

Before concluding my remarks about Ancient Medicine I must say something about snakes and snake charming with which it is intimately connected.

It is a very remarkable fact that in the early history of Greek medicine the dog also occupied a prominent place as a sacred animal and that they were trained to lick the sick to cure them. This popular superstition has existed in all ages and even to-day belief in its efficacy has not been destroyed by modern science. It is only natural then that the dog should figure as a companion of the God of Medicine in the Temple of Epidarus, but he disappeared little by little from the temples, giving place to the mysterious and silent serpent.

How it all came about is a mystery, but not more of a mystery than that snakes and semi-mythical personages should still remain the emblems and idols of a serious and scientific profession. The myths associated with the snake are as ridiculous as they are innumerable. For instance, they were believed to be able to draw from the earth the source of inspiration, the secrets of the future and the medicinal secrets of plants.

It is possible, however, that their great mystic power was mostly due to the visible periodic rejuvenation after the shedding of the old skin. This is probably why the snake was chosen as the emblem of health.

It is a curious fact that the snakes found in the vicinity of the temples were inoffensive, easily tamed and therefore easily employed to strike the imagination of sick people. In the Stelae at Epidaurus there are many examples of strange cures for even stranger maladies. Barren women naturally frequently appear and curiously enough a serpent seems to have provoked in some women what were called lewd dreams.

Aesculapius, the Roman God of Medicine, is always represented with his baton entwined by a serpent. As an example of the universal ignorance concerning this common emblem, it must be mentioned that it is frequently confounded with the Caduceus Wand of Mercury which is entwined with two serpents. This ludicrous error is often to be seen, especially in the United States where it appears not only in buildings but also on motor cars. The wand entwined with two serpents has nothing whatsoever to do with medicine and is, of course, the emblem of the God of Merchants, Thieves and Pick-pockets.

There is much difference of opinion concerning the claims put forward on behalf of certain tribes, mostly the Rifaee dervishes, that they can charm snakes. Anyone who seriously investigates the matter with an unbiased mind must admit that they do exercise some mysterious power over them. On the other hand, I have heard them described as impostors. But apart from instances of pure jugglery when live and venomous snakes appear to be swallowed, no one in my opinion has ever offered a satisfactory explanation of the most common and yet the most interesting of the performances of the snake charmers.

We are told in the Old Testament that the ancient Peylli in Cyrenaica possessed a secret art enabling them to secure themselves against the poison of serpents. Their powers must have been due to hypnotic influences and are of the greatest historic and biological interest. This peculiar power over snakes and some other animals still exists to-day but it is most in evidence among primitive tribes although it is by no means exclusively confined to them.

I once knew a doctor who put a cobra into a state of catalepsy in the Temple of Karnak. He was famous among keepers in Zoological Gardens for his hypnotic tricks with snakes, lizards, parrots, owls, bears and even big cats, all of whom he could throw into a state of lethargy. His performances provide positive evidence of the secret art that was fully recognized in ancient times.

The Ancient Egyptians possessed a similar power. We know of their success in taming wild animals, even snakes and crocodiles. This gift, if it can be so described, has been inherited by distinct tribes among the present inhabitants of the country. They make a living now as snake charmers and travel all over Egypt ridding houses of serpents, employing the following method on most occasions. Assuming an attitude of great mystery and concentration, the snake charmer strikes the wall at the opening of a snake's burrow with a palm stick or it may be a tuft of grass. At the same time he whistles or sings a monotonous refrain, adjuring the snake in the name of Allah to come forth. And sure enough the serpent does come forth, or if not he puts his hand into the hole and drags it out, sometimes being bitten in the process. I have often seen snakes dislodged from fissures in walls, burrows and dark chambers which no ordinary person would dare to enter.

The most successful snake charmer to-day in Egypt is Moussa (Moses) at Luxor. He is well known among the tourists for his marvellous and inexplicable exploits. In matters of this kind, however, I prefer to rely on my own judgment, formed after personal investigation and observation. I was lucky enough to have a good opportunity to make up my own mind on the subject when staying with a friend, the late Mr. Bowden Smith, at Damietta.

We heard of a snake charmer and decided to put him through a severe test. He arrived with his basket and stick and was carefully searched. We went in a direction quite unknown to him to a mound where there were some rat burrows. There we stripped him naked, leaving him with nothing but his palm stick. He walked round just like a retriever in the proximity of game, singing a peculiar monotonous song all the time. Suddenly he would put his stick or sometimes his hand into a hole in the ground or a tuft of grass and haul out a live snake. When he had finished, our basket contained six live snakes.

How can this be explained? Was he guided by a sense of smell extraordinarily developed? There certainly must be some real physical means of discovering snakes without seeing them, but what it is we do not know. It is just as difficult to comprehend reptilian psychology as the mysterious powers of snake charmers. Anyone who has watched a snake enticing a lizard before dining on it will readily understand that they themselves may be easily affected by hypnosis exercised by a more powerful organism.

XII

IN my long experience of the medical profession especially in foreign countries, I have often been amazed at the many mistaken ideas about doctors in the minds of the lay public. At all times we have received extravagant praise and even more extravagant censure. Bitter satire and criticism have been levelled at us throughout the ages. We have been accused by some of ignorance, hypocrisy and avarice, while others have praised us for our unselfishness, heroism and generosity.

Much of the criticism to-day seems to be directed against our so-called medical etiquette (which is largely a myth) and our alleged intolerance towards the army of unqualified or irregular practitioners who prey on a gullible public.

There may or may not be good reasons for the adverse criticism of doctors in general, but much of it would disappear if the golden rule of live and let live were more faithfully observed by individual members of the profession. But unfortunately when men are full of envy and jealousy, they are only too ready to disparage everything and everyone, conveniently forgetting that idle discussion of a single error committed by a colleague may work irrevocable injury to his reputation.

It is remarkable that some of the bitterest things said

against medicine and doctors have come from the mouths of doctors themselves. Perhaps in Bowen's famous phrase, they are too conscious of their general unworthiness not to extend this feeling to the noble art which they practise.

Maurice Reynaud has written that he has never insulted the physicians as much as they do each other. There are innumerable records of this animosity between various members of the profession in history. Molière has satirized for all time the bitter warfare which one school of medicine waged against another in France and laughed and mocked at their savage invectives. But such civil war inside the profession was nothing new. The immortal Hippocrates was the centre of even more violent disputes and calumny. As a matter of fact, he has never ceased to be so. Molière declared warfare on the pedantry of his time as exemplified by the schools of Paris and Montpellier and their burlesque quarrels. He holds up the tenets of both schools to ridicule. Montpellier accuses Paris of bleeding too much; Paris replies that Montpellier practises purgation with excess. Then Patin of Paris alludes to one of his Montpellier colleagues as ignorant, mercenary, infamous and a quack, which has quite a modern touch. Paris wrongly accuses Montpellier of having fled before the plague after having boasted that they had a cure for the scourge. Montpellier retorts, "you ought to have come forward with lemon juice, your scabious leaves and your famous lancet."

At this period it must be admitted that the medical profession did not command high respect. The majority of its members were treated then without any consideration. They were spoken to and spoken of as if they were menials. It was obligatory for a doctor to change his clothes before paying a professional visit, which shows what his patients really thought of him. Some may say that it is a pity this rule is not rigidly enforced to-day. At the same time, it should be pointed out that Molière's destructive criticism did not apply to all the doctors of his time but was directed for the most part against the Court physicians, their conditions, intrigues and rivalry. His strictures pleased the King himself and the well known works, *L'Amour Medicine* and *Le Malade Imaginaire*, were especially written as homage to His Majesty.

To come to still later times, in 1748 Quesnay, a physician of high standing, published an essay on the great quarrel reigning between physicians and surgeons. He begins by saying that the first point to be decided is whether these professions are useful or injurious to society, and whether they should be abolished or allowed to continue to exist. He was obviously sceptical as to the utility of drugs, for he points out that among the poor medical treatment is very simple, consisting of bleeding and the administration of tisanes, a few purgatives and very little else. This, he says, is all that really can be done and perhaps he was not far wrong.

It is related that when Lieutaud, first physician to Louis XVI, was near his end, his confessor wanted to assure himself that the dying man was in his right mind and plied him with questions concerning his belief in all the mysteries of religion. Wearied at last by so many interrogations, Lieutaud finally replied: "I believe in everything except medicine".

Professor Gregory told the following story in his Memorial to the Managers of the Royal Infirmary in Edinburgh in 1803.

"Of the many bitter sarcasms which I have heard of my own profession and professional brethren, one of the severest was that of a certain Dr. Garth on his deathbed. When one of his friends came to see him, he asked him what physician he would advise him to send for if he were taken ill himself, thinking that the learned doctor's professional opinion would be of great value to him. But all that Dr. Garth replied was: "Send for the nearest".

Such utterances, of course, must not be taken too seriously, but they are nevertheless indications of the state of mind which Du Maurier represented in a famous drawing many years ago. It showed an anxious wife trying to induce her sick husband, a doctor, to send for one of his colleagues and his definite refusal "because we all go in for thinking each other quacks". How I sympathize with that sentiment! We not only think each other quacks but sometimes act the part of quacks.

And yet the science of medicine has a right to the cabalistic for it came from Greece. Pliny says that for six hundred years the Romans got on very well without doctors and would have continued to do so had they not been imported from Greece.

Professional secrecy is one of the most striking of the principles that underlie the code of medical ethics. A physician should hold as inviolate any information imparted to him by his patient and such confidences should not be disclosed even in a Court of Justice. And how familiar we all are with people's eagerness to hear details concerning the illness of persons with whom they may only be slightly acquainted. There is no limit to which people will not go in their anxiety to probe the domestic affairs of their neighbours. It is thus all the more essential for there to be a strict code of professional secrecy among doctors. The sad and cruel consequences of the failure to observe this golden rule are well exemplified by the celebrated case of Lady Flora Hastings in the early part of the last century.

In 1839 Lady Flora was on duty at Court performing the functions of a lady-in-waiting to Queen Victoria, when her appearance suggested to some of her associates that she might be with child. One of them reported her suspicions to Sir James Clark, the Court physician, who at once accepted the insinuation as the truth. He interviewed her and intimated that she "must be privately married" or at least ought to be so. This Lady Flora indignantly denied and to vindicate her character demanded that she should be medically examined. Lord Melbourne reluctantly permitted this to take place and it at once established her chastity. Sir James Clark and Sir Charles Clark certified that there were no grounds for believing that pregnancy existed or ever had existed. Lady Flora only survived this terrible ordeal by a few months. If Sir James Clarke had only exercised that prudence and delicacy which should ever characterize the physician in dealing with such matters, if he had only been a little more alert and circumspect, he could have saved the lady and her friends much anguish and distress.

Another instance of the disastrous consequences of a doctor's tactless remarks is to be found in the noted case of Kitson v. Playfair and wife in 1896. In this case, Dr. Playfair told his wife that Mrs. Kitson had had a recent miscarriage although she had been away from her husband for considerably more than a year, her husband being Mrs. Playfair's brother. This Mr. Kitson was not prosperous and he received an allowance of £500 a year from his brother who discontinued it as a result of Dr. Playfair's unfortunate and damaging statement to his wife. At the trial, it was proved that a placenta might be retained in utero for more than a year after a miscarriage. The damages were assessed at £5,000 by the plaintiff but the jury awarded the unprecedented sum of £12,000, which was reduced by mutual consent to £9,200 in the end. The verdict strengthens the vital importance of a doctor preserving the confidence of his patients.

I had a very interesting experience in connection with the famous Maybrick case. I was determined to witness the trial, not on account of any desire to satisfy morbid curiosity, as is evidenced to-day in such a loathsome manner at murder and divorce trials, but because of the nature of the medical evidence which was extremely complicated. It was quite impossible, however, to obtain a ticket of admission. So I got a long blue envelope, filled it with paper and tied some red tape round it. With this in hand, I presented myself at St. George's Hall where the trial was taking place. I went through four doors well guarded by policemen and was only challenged at the last, but pointing to my legal document with an air of authority I got through without much difficulty. I heard the evidence of the accused as well as the speeches of the prosecuting and defending counsel.

Sir Charles Russel, as he then was, appeared to be oppressed by his responsibilities and did not excel himself, although he believed to the day of his death in the innocence of his unfortunate client.

There is a dangerous theory being fostered just now that nobody can keep well or when ill get well without medical advice and that such advice will be more effective if the physician happens to have many titled patients. It is extraordinary how this strange idea thrives in what is supposed to be a democractic age. Such a theory is equivalent to the incantations used by the witch doctors to impress their patients. Like them, its only effect can be one of suggestion and that in both cases seems to be extraordinarily powerful. The potency of the incantation of "I am Lord Timbuctoo's doctor" cannot be denied. Is it any wonder that there should be undignified intrigue for the position of medical attendant to the titled gods?

I have always found the purely French and Italian doctors correct in their professional conduct, and I can say the same with regard to the Egyptians, some of whom are very intelligent and proficient in their work.

Petrarch said: "Shun the physician who is eminent not for his knowledge but solely for his powers of speech, as you would a lurking assassin or a poisoner". And some Greek writer said that "a prattling physician is another disease to a sick person". Whether this is true or not must be left to everyone's experience. I certainly do not think myself that a doctor's first duty is to be sombre, sepulchral and silent. On the other hand, the loquacious type has its peculiarities. I knew a fine specimen of this kind of doctor some years ago. It was said at the time that he did not possess a proper diploma but such were his powers of persuasion that it made no difference to the number of his patients. He was a past master in the art of giving the right impression. He used to drive about in a smart Victoria always reading, or rather pretending to do so. At night he had two candles fixed up in the back of his carriage so as to be able to continue his fictitious studies. It impressed people enormously. On all sides you heard the remark: "Poor doctor, he never gets a moment to himself, he always has to be preparing for his next difficult case". The sympathy was redoubled when he was called out of church which frequently happened. He had patients amongst all sorts of people including royalty who thought a great deal of him for he was a most accomplished buffoon. Sometimes he disappeared and it was rumoured that he had gone to Paris or Vienna to see some distinguished personage dangerously ill but the truth was far less impressive and far more romantic if such sordid adventures can be called so. He gave enormous doses of medicines and prescribed every new medicine as soon as it was announced. This greatly impressed patients and chemists who ignored the fact that the majority of such drugs have a very short life.

But the most brazen piece of effrontery I have ever encountered happened during the serious illness of the late King George some years ago. A certain local doctor suddenly disappeared and I soon heard the rumour that he had been called to London in consultation with the King's doctors. Many people actually believed it and sometime afterwards a highly intelligent American visitor mentioned to me what a wonderful physician this man must be to be called all the way to London in connection with the King's illness. I soon opened his eyes to the truth. The most amazing part of the whole episode was the way the doctor in question took advantage afterwards of this skilfully engineered rumour. Many people spoke to him about the "Royal Consultation" and asked him questions about it but they always received the same reply : "I would rather not discuss the matter".

Speaking of consultations, some patients may have heard of the word Dichotomy without knowing what it means. It sounds well but in the medical world it signifies the base transaction of the division of the consultant's fees with the practitioner who called him in consultation. It is backsheesh pure and simple but according to reports in the medical journals it is a growing industry. I have been offered fifty per cent for my surgical work myself but I never saw my way to accepting such tempting offers.

I believe many practitioners are in the habit of falling over each other in their anxiety to land big fish in the way of millionaires. I have met more than one of the fraternity and it occasioned me no surprise that they are successful in accumulating so much sordid gold.

Mammon is contemptible at any time but when associated with unbounded wealth is contemptible to a degree. Perhaps the worst case was one that happened in Cairo before the war. A titled personage reputed to be worth millions was travelling with a party of guests. One of them, a titled lady, was taken seriously ill. I diagnosed a fatal disease and had her removed to Miss Jameson's Nursing Home. When she was well enough to travel, I accompanied her to Port Said and placed her under the charge of the ship's doctor. The lady, long since dead, was in comparatively poor circumstances and as my attendance extended over several weeks, I naturally sent my memorandum for fees to the millionaire but payment was refused.

But all millionaires are not so parsimonious and I am happy to recall a long and pleasant association with such well known men as Mr. Solly Joel and Mr. Cyrus McCormick whose generosity well compensates for the meanness of other wealthy men.

Many amusing situations frequently arise with foreign doctors of all nationalities who cannot speak English with patients who only speak that language. The doctor generally greets his victim with a "good morning" in a rasping voice, while the Englishman not to be outdone replies with an equally effective accent "bonjour" or "bon giorno" as the case may be. The doctor then explodes in a torrent of French (or Italian) to which the Englishman calmly replies in English, but neither of them understand a word of what the other is saying. At last the poor patient in desperation says: "Je suis malade". "Oui, oui, yes, yes" replies the doctor. Then comes another torrent of unintelligible French to which the patient again replies in his own language. At last he has an inspiration and places his hand on his chest or on whatever part of his anatomy he imagines to be the seat of his illness and says briefly: "Ici!" The necessary garment is removed and the doctor with a loud and significant grunt of "Ooh, aah, oui, oui, yes," makes his

diagnosis and writes a prescription in French to be translated with the aid of a dictionary by the patient if he
survives long enough to do so. The doctor then says:
"Good morning, Mister" and the patient says: "Bonjour,
Monsieur".

Of all the strange practitioners, qualified and unqualified, who have adorned the profession in every
country and in every age, I doubt if it would be possible
to find a more curious individual than Mr. Roger Giles,
a surgeon, whose remarkable sign board was discovered
in a Cornish village and is now in the possession of the
Horniman Museum, London. Mr. Giles practised as
late as the last century and advertised himself in the
following manner.

ROGER GILES SURGIN

Parish Clark & Skulemaster, Groser & Hundertaker,
Respectably Informs Ladys & Gentlemen That He Drors
Teef Without Wateing a Minit. Applies Laches Every
Hour. Blisters On the Lowest Tarms and Visicks For A
Penny A Peace. He Sells Godfather's Kordales. Kuts
Corns & Bunyons. Doctors Hosses, Clips Donkies
Wance A Munth & Hundertakes To Luke After Every
Bodies Nayls By The Ear. Joes-Harps, Penny Wissels,
Brass Canelsticks, Fryinpans & Other Moozikal Hinstru-
ments Hat Grately Reydoosed Figers. Young Ladys &
Gentlemen Larnes Their Garrmur And Langeeudge In
The Puritest Manner. Also Grate Care Taken Of Their
Morrels & Spellin. Also Zarm-Zinging, Tayching The
Base Vial & All Other Zorts Of Fancy Works Quadrils
Pokers Weazels & All Country Dances Tort At Home &
Abroad At Perfekshun. Perfumery & Snuff In All Its

Branches. As Times Is Cruel Bad I Begs To Tell Ee That I Has Just Beginned To Sell All Sorts Of Stashonary Ware. Cox, Hens, Vouls, Pigs And All Other Kind Of Poultry. Blackin-Brishes, Henrrins, Coles, Scrubbing Brishes, Traykel And Godly Books And Bibles. Mise Traps, Brick Dist, Whisker Seeds. Morrel Pokkeran-kechers. And All Zorts of Swatemaits Including Taters, Sassages And Other Gardenstuff. Bakky, Zizzars, Lamp Oyle, Tay, Kittles And Other Intoxzikatin Likkers. A Dale Of Fruit, Hats, Zongs, Hareoyle. Pattins. Bukkits. Grindstones and Other Aitables. Korn & Bunyon Zalve & All Hardware. I Has Laid In a Large Assortment Of Trype, Dog Mate, Lollipops, Ginger Beer, Matches & Other Pickles. Such As Hepsom, Salts, Hoysters. Windzer Sope. Anzetrar. Old Rags Bort And Sold Here And Nowhere Else. Newlayd Heggs By Me Robert Giles. Zinging Burdes Keeped Sich As Howls, Donkies, Payrox. Lobsters. Crickets. Also A Stock Of A Cele-brated Brayder. Itayches. Gography. Rithmetic. Cow-sticks. Jimnasticks And Other Chynesstricks. Gode Save Thee Kinge."

Unfortunately there is no record to say whether he was as successful a doctor as he was publicity agent. In that respect, he lived a little too soon. Now he would have made his fortune with such an undoubted gift for advertising unmarketable goods.

It is not to be wondered at that the unthinking public has never had a very high opinion of the medical pro-fession. On the other hand, the thinking part has held individual practitioners in the highest esteem. Diogenes went out with a candle to find an honest man, but failed.

But would his search have been such a failure if he had encountered some members of the medical profession? A Chinese writer has said that a doctor should be square, his knowledge round, his gall bladder large and his heart small. But whatever view may be taken of the profession, it cannot be denied that a doctor is the only man in these troublous times, who continues to soothe pain and labour unremittingly in his search for means to allay the sufferings of humanity, frequently without any hope of pecuniary reward. As Stephan Page said: "If a doctor's life may not be a divine vocation, then no life is a vocation and nothing is divine".

I have already alluded to several well known Liverpool practitioners. There are some others worthy of mention. "Bob Jones" at that period was not much more than a "club doctor" but he had inherited the great prestige attached to a family of bone-setters. His uncle, Mr. Thomas (the inventor of the famous splint) had an enormous practice especially among the working classes. His unique get up always seated in the same attitude in a matchless barouche was one of the most familiar sights in the Liverpool streets in those days. Everyone recognized Thomas the Bone-setter at first sight.

"Bob Jones" drove a very smart pair of cobs, always travelling at such a rapid pace that it would take a modern road-hog all his time to keep up with him. Of course no one ever dreamed then that he would end as Sir Robert Jones (Bart). He was certainly one of the most famous orthopædic surgeons of his time and did wonderful work for cripples and especially for disabled soldiers during the war. The dominant element that then ruled the Royal Infirmary must have had some intuition concerning the young surgeon, for it was common knowledge at one time that they did not look on him with very friendly eyes.

Another practitioner who demands mention is Dr. James Barr, now Sir James Barr. It was always a great treat to hear his stentorian voice with its pronounced Ulster accent assert itself at medical meetings. As a prison doctor, Dr. Barr was sent to Ireland during the troubles by Mr. Arthur Balfour to investigate some cases then very much discussed. As a reward for his services, he soon blossomed forth as "Sir James".

I believe it is useful for a doctor "to have a handle to his name", for there are always many obsequious parasites to be found. I was once the fortunate witness of a very amusing incident, by way of illustration. Three Liverpool ladies were discussing doctors in a tram. One of them said: "Sir James said that I was not to eat strawberries;" the other said: "Sir James told me on no account to eat gooseberries"; while the third, not to be outdone, said: "Sir James told me to eat herrings as they contain calcium which is essential for a healthy existence". Sir James has now reached an advanced age but as he stated some years ago that he was in excellent health, it is to be hoped that he will still continue to amuse and instruct us.

We have still happily with us another estimable practitioner and brilliant surgeon, Mr. Frank T. Paul. He deserves to be mentioned apart from anything else for his ably expressed views (which I fully share) concerning the cause of the terrible scourge of cancer, which is continually increasing in spite of the enormous sums fruitlessly spent on research.

Mr. Paul regards over-nutrition and over-sexed conditions as the cause of cancer, and emphasizes the undoubted fact that it is very rare or quite unknown in the really wild life of any class of animal, while it is common and becoming increasingly common in man and all domesticated animals encouraged to lead a life based on human habits.

This leads one, in looking for the cause, to believe that we should study the influence of habits. If we could see back to the earliest stage of the wild life of man when he had to search and fight for his food in order to live and when his sex function only came into use when definitely required for procreation, should we find that he ever suffered from cancer? Certainly not; nor is there to-day any cancer among the primitive tribes in any part of Africa visited by me. Why then are such patent facts ignored, and search made for an evolutionary cause, not a germ?

I have the most pleasant recollections of Sir Clifford Allbutt of Leeds, truly the "beloved physician", always helpful and considerate. His learning was profound and as a clinician he was amongst the very ablest of his generation. I often picture Hippocrates as another clinician similar to Clifford Allbutt and in saying that, I feel I am paying a great compliment to both of them. He was a credit to the Leeds School that is always the first among provincial centres of medical education.

With his name should be linked that of Berkeley Moyniham, equally a credit to the Leeds School and the great profession which he adorned. I last saw him at the International Medical Congress in Cairo in 1934.

Lord Moyniham combined the qualities of a great surgeon, a great scholar and a great orator, but most wonderful of all was his great heart full of kindness and sympathy.

About Lord Dawson it is unnecessary to say much. He is rightly looked upon by practitioners in Great Britain as a great leader, a great clinician and a wise counsellor.

Other doctors who have made a lasting impression on me include Sir Victor Horsley who was a genius and perhaps the greatest brain surgeon of all times; Mr. Victor Bonney, still happily with us, a quiet and unassuming man but a very great surgeon; Sir William Stokes, one of the most brilliant operators I have ever seen and whose tragic death in South Africa during the Boer War was a great loss to the Dublin School, and Professor Grocco, the famous clinician.

But doctors have their failings like the rest of the world. In a play recently produced in Paris, one of the characters was a hooligan who passed himself off as a doctor in order to get himself out of a tight place, but he went to sleep on the breast of the patient whom he was pretending to ausculate. However improbable this may seem, the thing has actually happened. About a year before his death, Professor Potain was called to a man suffering from severe bronchitis. The physician asked to be left alone with his patient and proceeded to ausculate his chest, asking him to count aloud. Waiting behind the door for the verdict of the oracle, the anxious wife was surprised at the length of the consultation and at last went in to see what was the matter. She found the doctor asleep on the breast of her husband who was steadily counting and had nearly reached five hundred.

This reminds me of the doctor who was called to attend a patient while he was in the midst of a game of cribbage one night after a dinner which he must have thoroughly enjoyed in every way. He tried to count the patient's pulse and got on well enough until he reached the critical number of fifteen. Then he proceeded to say: "Fifteen two, fifteen four, one for his nob," and so on.

A well known American physician figured in another story of a doctor going to sleep while examining a case. He had been recommended to a lady with a warning as to his temper when suddenly aroused—as the French say, *il avait le reveil brutal*. He went to her for the first time when he was tired out. Having to make an examination, he found the bed too tempting as a resting place for his head and went to sleep in that somewhat abnormal position. The unfortunate lady remembered the warning that she had received and was afraid to move or call for help. How long the doctor's slumbers lasted is not recorded but there is no doubt that the lady spoke the truth when she described the subsequent situation as "very awkward".

A story is told of a celebrated physician called in to examine Joseph II of Austria. The doctor was either absent-minded or overawed by being brought into such close contact with an Emperor even in bed. Putting his hand under the bedclothes to feel his patient's pulse, he seized what he thought was his wrist but was in reality another part of the Imperial person. His Majesty called his attention to the fact in the gracious words: "Erras, amice. Hoc est notre Imperiale membrum." What the physician's feelings were is not recorded. One must, however, admire the tact with which the Emperor dealt with a delicate situation.

But to return to more serious subjects. From what I have already written, it can easily be surmised that I have not much respect for the medical knowledge of the Ancient Egyptians, but at the same time I should be very sorry to join in the universal chorus of contempt and derision concerning their invocations and incantations.

They were a very religious people and appeals made to the gods, whom they deeply reverenced, must have profoundly affected their minds by the mere influence of suggestion, acting in the same way as do certain inoculations and vaccines to-day, not forgetting what is called personality and the bedside manner.

Ancient medicine was mental and the magic physicians were clever enough to realize that many unhealthy conditions could be greatly benefited through mental influences. But otherwise the Medical Art of the Ancients was strangled in the shackles of the greatest superstition and charlatanism from which some people may say it has never been able completely to free itself. The immortal Hippocrates, the founder of scientific medicine, was the first to attempt reform and to curb the evil influences of the priest physicians of the period, in which he partly succeeded in doing after a desperate struggle.

A few years ago I visited Cos and the site of the famous school in the precincts of the Temple of Aesculapius now in ruins. In a small piazza in the modern town, there is a very ancient plane called The Plane Tree of Hippocrates. Under its spreading branches, the illustrious master is said to have lectured to his pupils. There is a tablet on the tree inscribed with the words of the famous Hippocratic Oath, an oath which should be sworn by every medical person on presentation of his or her degree or diploma.

Before the practices of the Ancient are too strongly condemned, however, it would be well to consider a little the fallacies and absurdities associated with orthodox medical practice in much more recent times. I remember when antisepsis was first introduced and the fury of its opponents. Much of the teaching of the period is now discarded and we no longer see the carbolic acid spray emitting its destructive essence on germs, real or imaginary, benign or malignant. The credit for this theory is popularly ascribed to Lord Lister but the first to urge the gospel of personal and hospital cleanliness in this country was in reality the late Sir Edwin Chadwick who only earned the obloquy of his contemporaries.

To Semmelweis of Budapest, however, should be attributed the credit of exposing the dangers of dirt. He assailed filthy practices and was furiously assailed in his turn by his contemporaries who scoffed at him and his fads. No less an authority than Dr. Klein, in order to repudiate and discredit Semmelweis, continued to demonstrate on the cadaver and then to go straight to the lying-in chamber with unwashed hands. It seems almost unbelievable now that the orthodox herd should have sided with him as they did. And all this hatred, slander and ignorance, nurtured on dirt, happened not longer ago than the last century.

Now let us turn to the microbes themselves. We are asked to believe that most of our troubles and diseases are due to malevolent germs. We are told that the world is swarming with specific organisms going about seeking whom they may devour, and acting in the same mysterious way as the evil spirits of the Ancients or the afreets of modern Egypt.

As the late Dr. Crookshank said, "these views have so impressed themselves upon the profession that it will be a difficult struggle before what may be called the functional view-point can be re-established, and we come to see that many diseased states, so far as they have a bacteriological origin, are reactions between the body of the host and organisms which normally are harmless but which turn 'bolshevik' and become mischievous when the functional integrity of the host weakens or is perverted." That is the crux of the whole matter. We must again place reliance on natural agencies and defences. Fortunately the Hippocratic principles of fresh air and sunlight have once more triumphed. It seems almost incredible that fresh air, pure water, sunlight, the liberal use of soap and water and physical exercises should ever have been looked upon as dreadful superstitions and the advocates of these laws of healthy living considered quacks and cranks. But such indeed was the case not so very many years ago.

Although there has been much progress since the days of Hippocrates, Galen and Sydenham, their inductions, founded on clinical experience and the close study of natural phenomena including temperament, climate, constitution and environment, have remained as guides worthy of imitation by physicians of every age, with the result that the tendency to follow nature and nature's methods is becoming more and more apparent to-day.

We hear much now of psycho-analysis and the new psychology. In fact, the whole Freudian system is now so vulgarized that the phraseology has entered into the everyday language of ordinary people. They flippantly allude to their complexes and behaviourism, not only as if they knew what they were talking about which they almost invariably do not, but also as if such speculations were founded on established scientific facts which they most certainly are not.

The whole theory of the subconscious or unconscious has completely changed of recent years but the urge of sex which was the only urge recognized in the beginning, appealed enormously to the morbid herd and the new science received an enormous impetus followed by the inevitable reaction. Much of the disrepute into which the new psychology has fallen is partly due to the confused statements of its supporters and to the activities of numerous charlatans who exploit it for commercial purposes.

As a matter of fact, very few qualified practitioners practise psycho-analysis; if they did, perhaps its dangerous ill effects might be more noticeable. As might only be expected, behaviourism and all it stands for has received more attention in America than anywhere else. Such being the case, the views of some leading American neurologists cannot be without interest.

Dr. William White of Washington believes that Freud's greatness lies in his having evolved an entirely new point of view and a new method which

266

will ultimately discard the errors incidental to its present employment and discover the facts which it is capable of discovering just like any other scientific method.

Dr. Frederick Peterson of New York emphatically declares that Freudianism is a voodoo religion characterized by obscene rites and human sacrifices. He adds that psycho-analysis has in many cases caused mental aberration, insanity or suicide and that much of the work of the neurologists to-day consists of the reconstruction of the unfortunate victims of Freudianism.

This is a very serious indictment from a leading neurologist, but I doubt if it will have much effect, for one of the most astonishing characteristics of this machine age is its ability to suffer fools gladly.

When I first visited the African continent, I was very much struck by the remarkable toilettes of the native women. Garish designs disfigured the face and lips, feet and hands. Finger nails and toe nails were heavily dyed with henna or other pigment. Eyebrows were specially treated by depilation, eyelashes by kohl and other medicaments were also used for the eyes themselves. Large flat rings were suspended from one nostril. The one object and aim seemed to be to alter the natural appearance as much as possible.

Less than a generation ago no one in his senses would have predicted that so-called civilized women, young and old, would imitate the barbaric customs and practices of their native sisters.

It is extremely distasteful to have such unnatural exhibitions constantly before one's eyes but there is no escaping them. This chemical decoration of the female face is to be seen everywhere. Quite apart from the question of æsthetics, very serious objections can be raised on medical grounds against such practices. They are most deleterious to the skin, especially the delicate mucous membrane lining the lips, and it would not be at all surprising if malignant disease was sometimes the result of such constant irritation. Another objection is that it is now quite impossible to diagnose certain conditions from the facial appearance. The paint and cosmetics effectually conceal the outward manifestation of indifferent health and certain diseases. The depilation of the eyebrows likewise prevents a correct interpretation of certain signs implying something wrong with the glands of internal secretions, now recognized of vital importance in matters of health.

Another remarkable revival of barbaric instincts is the craze for tinting beautiful white skins with special dyes and causing deep pigmentation by exposing them to the rays of the sun after lubrication with oil, in actual imitation of the dark skins of native women. This practice is very common among young girls in Mediterranean steamers who expose their unpicturesque bodies without the slightest regard for other people's feelings.

There are certainly many affinities between the women of the present generation and their savage sisters. The music and dancing in which they delight originated among primitive people and would not have been tolerated in civilized society a generation ago. But now jazz bands, composed entirely of American negroes, are engaged for the season at famous hotels frequented by the "quality". Their antics, songs and music are obviously highly appreciated, but they are all highly reminiscent of the bush and the orgies that take place in savage lands. The dancing excels in licentiousness and vulgarity anything to be witnessed among primitive tribes. Even the names of the dances are negroid and vulgar. But while emphasizing the striking resemblances between modern and savage practices, there is one striking difference which hardly redounds to the reputation of the modern white man and woman.

The ancestral worship, which has existed from time immemorial among primitive tribes, is still as strong as ever to-day. And the same can be said of tribal and family honour. It is still considered a sacred duty to uphold the honour and interests of the tribe and family. When such hereditary obligations are violated, crimes are of frequent occurrence.

The very reverse is the case among so-called civilized people to-day. The virtues or instincts of primitive races, whichever you prefer to call them, are being completely neglected. For instance, the women and girls who come to Cairo during the season show not the slightest respect for their ancestors, tribe, clan or family. On the contrary, their behaviour is often a disgrace to their ancestors, their country and their sex. I have seen love letters written by them to low class natives, couched in the most endearing terms. The letters are shamelessly signed and often bear the signature of well known and respected families. Not only do these women fall victims to the attractions of coloured illiterates themselves, but they actually give their female friends letters of introduction to these natives to be used by them when they visit the country. Depravity and degeneracy of this kind are by no means uncommon and thoughtful people must realize that it forms a serious menace to the prestige of the white race.

But after all, are the women solely to blame for the present day shameless behaviour and hideous exhibition of cosmetics? Surely men need not wait until women have rings in their nostrils to assert their authority? Or are the men of to-day too effeminate to discriminate between good and evil, the vulgar and the refined, the natural and the unnatural? The complacency with which young men view the variegated pictures of their female friends and their behaviour is one of the most remarkable phases of our social life. There is but one explanation: their physical bodies are also essentially primitive while their souls are possessed by paganism.

The fact that all ancient civilizations have disappeared leaving nothing behind them except the survival of the most ancient religious cult, ancestor worship, which itself is decaying among many civilized races, does not lend much support to the theory of evolution. History leaves us with two fundamental truths; that all known civilization is traceable to the training and teaching which one generation communicates to another, the parents teaching the children, and that we have positively no knowledge of any single tribe who have fallen into barbarism ever rising out of it by themselves.

The philosophers of the East tell us humanity progresses in cycles, rising from barbarism to civilization and then falling back again to its original state. The present condition of civilized Europe certainly supports this Eastern theory. It is undeniable that it would be easy to find at all periods among primitive races witch doctors, sheiks, fakirs and puberty teachers with far more natural intelligence than many specialists and savants of great repute in the modern world. But no one except insular scientists and anthropologists would assert that the average intelligence of primitive races was higher than cultured and civilized people to-day, even when admitting that the cranial capacity of the prehistoric Cave Man was not inferior to ours. And yet the following views were expressed at a recent meeting of the Anthropological Section of the British Association:

"The average intelligence of man to-day is less than that of the pre-human at the end of the Hunting Period thousands of years ago. If the tailed monkeys had not taken to hunting, we should not have been here to-day. The standard of intelligence has been retrogressive since the beginning of the civilized period of the world. Polygamy has been largely responsible for the super average intelligence that exists to-day. When our ancestors left the trees and entered upon the terrestrial phase, they had to find more food and guard against terrestrial enemies, which accounted for their increased size. In some respects, the hunting phase was the most wonderful period in the history of our planet, for it saw the transformation of apes into men. But for the fact that our ancestors took to hunting, we should not be here to-day."

According to such extraordinary views, it may be inferred that the tailed monkeys are responsible for our acquisitive instincts as well as most of our present miseries. It seems to have escaped notice that this wonderful hunting period must also have been a most comic one. Imagine the tailed monkey slowly losing his tail and his hairy covering mysteriously disappearing and being replaced by white, black, yellow or red skin, while the very limited vocabulary with which he is still endowed was transformed into intelligible language.

Prehistoric history is still in its infancy. We know little about the laws that govern the modification of the skeleton, the slow or sudden modification of races or the speed at which sedimentation takes place. And yet we are told that the earth is millions of years old! And with all the barrenness of our knowledge, we have the pretension to write an authentic history of the human species distributed in the surface of the earth. Even our long cherished belief that the colour and character of different races are due to climatic conditions is now said to be a fallacy. We are asked to believe that the distinctive racial uniform is due to the glands of internal secretion. These glands certainly regulate growth and character but we are not told why they should act differently under different climatic conditions.

When Darwin visited the Galapagos Islands, he started one of the grandest generalizations in the history of science, and yet he knew nothing about these glands, all of which have an important bearing on the theory of evolution.

The pituitary gland produces giants among human beings, and under certain circumstances dwarfs also, yet this gland was considered by Darwin and his successors for a long time a vestigial organ devoid of all function. We know now that other glands almost completely control the entire reproductive development but their functions were practically unknown to the Darwinian school of thought.

We are told by the evolutionists that according to the laws of heredity, all natural variations are inherited. This may apply to primitive man, but when we come to civilized races, difficulties at once arise. How are the variations among such communities to be explained and do they tend, as is maintained, towards a high racial excellence? It is only by organized research among primitive tribes that an explanation will be found for such complex problems. Perhaps if they were a little better understood, we should take a more cheerful and hopeful view of the challenge of Neo-paganism with which the world is confronted to-day in its most insolent and barbaric form.

We are so obsessed with the strange doctrine of Simian descent that we assume that the study of race itself can teach us nothing, conveniently forgetting the fact that the famous doctrine shows signs of suffering the same fate as all such hypotheses, for few so-called scientific theories last for more than half a century. In spite of the geologist, the anthropologist and the periodic discovery of "wonderful skulls and skeletons more or less thirty thousand years old" in different parts of the world, the origin of man remains as profound a mystery as ever, unless we are foolish enough to be impressed by the latest theory put forward by a serious scientist when discussing what is called cosmic radiation. Professor J. B. S. Haldane, the eminent scientist, has said that many of the most cherished scientific theories contain so much falsehood as to deserve the title of myths. He believes that the biological theory (Darwinism) is equally riddled with falsehoods.

It is clear that since the beginning of the earth, a veritable progress in organisms can be observed. There is an evolution, but the precise nature of the evolution is unknown. It is only a question of time and it will no longer be tenable to uphold the Darwinian theory. The belief in mutations or sudden changes is gaining strength. This in itself when applied to man is a negation of the Darwinian hypothesis. Such a view receives support from present day events. At least three countries in Europe alone have fallen back into a state of semi-barbarism within a comparatively short space of time. Unless something happens to revive their sanity, the retrogression will undoubtedly proceed still further and eventually end in a degraded form of paganism.

In all such futile discussions, one predominant fact appears generally to be ignored: no matter how remotely we probe into the past, man is always found to be imbued with intelligence and religious beliefs whose common factor was, and is, ancestor worship. This cult dates as far back as the stone age, perhaps the most degraded age in the history of mankind, and very probably to a much earlier period when the human species was very different from what it is to-day.

Of all the conclusions forced upon me by my life as a doctor in Africa, none is stronger than this. And to have arrived at such a conclusion, I do not think I have laboured in vain. I should have liked to discuss more fully Ancient Egyptian Medicine, but I fear it is too esoteric a subject for the general public. I think I have said enough, however, to show that in the whole range of medical practice, there is not one single observation, discovery or form of treatment worthy of notice that has descended to us from Ancient Egypt. But if only for their knowledge of the therapeutic possibilities of suggestions in their own peculiar environment, these ancient practitioners do not altogether deserve the contempt expressed for their incantations and incubation sleep by the modern doctor, who has been brought up to treat sick people suffering from diseases that originate and have been named in the laboratory.

The ancient physicians, the sheiks, fikies and witch doctors and even the old hags who officiate in the awful Zaar, all treat sick people without knowing the names of their diseases. For this purpose, they use the most potent curative agents which the laboratory doctor does not understand, and they unquestionably obtain many satisfactory results and even astounding cures far more frequently than is generally admitted.

Even now it is impossible to form a really just estimate of the value of Ancient Egyptian Medicine owing to the scanty material at our disposal and the great difficulties of translation of what documents we have. But the same vagueness and even ignorance exists concerning the commonplace usages of the people in those early times.

Take the Ank or the Sign of Life which we see everywhere. No one can tell us the significance of this universal sign, although it is as old as Egyptian civilization. We see the oldest known midwives, the goddesses Ta Urt and Meskhenet, the former with her characteristic emblem of the Sa but sometimes represented with the Ank also, while the latter is depicted with the two symbols of the Ank and the Tet. It is remarkable that the early Christians when first converted discarded all the pagan symbols except the Ank. But it was adopted in the

East instead of the Cross and is mentioned in Ezekiel as the mark Tau set upon the forehead of the men "who were to be preserved alive".

The old inscription of the Christians in the great oasis is headed by the symbol, and it has been found on some of the monuments in Rome, while Wickersheimer, one of the oldest inhabitants of Munich, stated in 1910 that he had seen the sign in front of many of the houses in that city.

And yet, notwithstanding its great antiquity and its universal adoption, no Egyptologists can tell us for certain the object which the sign represented. It is said to be a conventional representation of some organs of the body connected with procreation. But the explanation generally accepted appears to be that the Crux Ansata was the symbol or emblem of life in Egypt, combining the generative organ, Phallus and Yoni. On the other hand, Budge says that the object represented by this amulet is unknown, and that of all the suggestions which have been made concerning it none is more unlikely than that which would give it a phallic origin. The most remarkable symbolical representation I have seen of this sign is an illustration where Thoth and Horus are depicted sprinkling water upon Pharaoh, saying at the same time: "Thou art pure; thou art pure again."

The true meaning of the Tet is likewise unknown. Although a symbol of the highest religious importance, no one can say what it meant originally. In Busiris, Osiris was worshipped under a strange figure of a pillar. This pillar is said to represent the tree trunk where Isis concealed the dead body of her husband Osiris and the cross bars the four cardinal points. On the other hand, others have asserted that this great religious symbol was simply a Nilometer, but in all probability it was a wooden fetish, set up for adoration, and like all other fetishes inexplicable.

The Swastika was invented by the Aryan races and means lucky. Curiously enough it was sometimes used as the equivalent of the cross which has nothing to do with its wide use in Germany to-day. It cannot, however, be considered a Christian symbol as it is to be found everywhere, even on the statues of Buddha. It is very frequently encountered in the East and is a common design on Eastern rugs. I do not suppose it was this fact which persuaded Hitler to put the symbol on the German national flag, but there are many who suggest that it will suffer in time the same treatment as the rugs. It is strange how these old pagan customs or emblems are being resuscitated. There are many views concerning the Swastika but that generally accepted is that it represents the solar system.

To give some idea of these strange people, the Egyptians, about whom so much nonsense has been written, let us consider the scarabs to be seen everywhere. The amulet of the heart, always considered of the first importance, was made in the form of a scarab from a very early date. When the physical heart was taken away for mummification, a substitute was necessary. A stone heart being only stone after all and the beetle or scarab being a very remarkable insect, the figure of the insect was adopted and in this way the scarab originated. Not only was it believed that the physical heart would be protected but also that new life would be given through the inherent qualities of the beetle to the person to whose body it was attached. The scarab was the type and symbol of the god Khepern, the invisible power of creation which propelled the sun across the sky. The fact that the scarab or beetle flies during the hottest part of the day and rolls the excremental matter in which its eggs are enclosed, has led to a comparison with the sun itself, and the act of rolling the ball gave the insect the name of Khepern, meaning he who rolls. The sun contains the germs of life, so also does the excremental ball with its eggs. The god Khepern also represented inert but living matter which was about to begin a course of existence. At a very early period he was considered the god of resurrection, and since the scarab was identified with him the insect became at once the symbol of the god.

Before leaving Ancient Egypt, it may be a consolation to the present day inhabitants of the country in the midst of their miseries and many troubles to remember that similar conditions existed four thousand years ago. An Ancient Egyptian Priest of Heliopolis in the twelfth dynasty thus expressed his bitter disillusionment in contemplating human unworthiness and the social miseries of his time:

"I squeeze out my breast for what is in it in dislodging all that I say; for it is but to repeat what has already been said, transformations go on, it is not like last year, one year is more burdensome than the last. Righteousness is cast out, iniquity is in the council hall, the land is in distress. All men are under wrongs. As for respect, an end is made of it. Nobody is free from evil, all men alike do it. There is none so wise that he perceives, and none so angry that he speaks. Manifold is the burden upon thee."

Nearly the whole world would join in this lament now with the unhappy old priest who in his misery appealed to his heart as a personal friend to help and encourage him.

Is the present state of civilization going to survive and thus prove an exception to the fate of many historic civilizations in the past?

There never was a time perhaps in the history of the world when so many unthinking people were influenced more by so-called intellectuals. As many of these guides desire to be considered atheists and Bolsheviks, it would appear at first sight as if their power for mischief were very great. And so it is, but not perhaps to the extent popularly imagined.

The immortality of the soul may be scoffed at as a primitive superstition, as one of these intellectuals said, adding that men die but man never dies and that he therefore believed that man is immortal but not men. But this superstition like many others rests on a solid foundation, and belief in its truth is deeply impregnated in the bone, marrow and tissues of countless persons. I might appropriately mention two incidents which quite recently came within my personal knowledge and for the truth of which I can vouch.

A well known and highly popular man was seized in a chemist's shop with what was considered a fatal illness. Burial took place according to the regulations within twenty-four hours. He appeared to his widow and said: "I am not dead," and shortly afterwards re-appeared and said: "I am now dead". The poor widow was naturally distracted and insisted on having the coffin opened. When this was done, it was found that the husband had unmistakably turned over on one side. There was no question but that burial had taken place before life was extinct. With the other questions involved, I have nothing to say.

The other incident was told to me by a highly educated man of strong and exemplary character who lost his only son in the war. He received a letter from him saying that he was coming home on leave on a certain date. He went to the station to meet him and saw a carriage window open, his son appear at it and almost simultaneously vanish again. He received a letter the same day from the War Office saying that his son had been killed.

It is strange how even some modern self-constituted leaders of thought cannot get away from primitive beliefs, although no doubt they would deeply resent any such implication. But what other explanation can be offered?

Their creed, consciously or unconsciously, seems to be to live for the race. It is doubtless very beautiful in theory but is it not a reversion to the great primitive religion of totemism, the most ancient of all beliefs? It is perhaps more comprehensive, for whereas formerly the totem symbolized the worship and protection of the tribe, to-day its intellectual followers include the collective souls and bodies of the whole race, for it should be emphasized that their instincts are distinctly non-tribal. And it is because of this anti-tribal animus that their power for mischief is neutralized. And yet with all this nonsense that is written about the race, no man can really say to which race he belongs, unless like Pooh Bah he can trace his ancestry back to a semi-fluid substance called protoplasm, the basis of life.

I do not wish to make any apocalyptic prophecies about the near future, but it would be extremely foolish to ignore current events. With the profound and incomprehensible mutation, individual and racial, the political jealousies, hatreds and assassinations, the fiasco of international conferences, the supreme fiasco of Geneva, the grave economic crisis with the prospect that millions of men are destined to be permanently unemployed, the almost universal corruption and dishonesty and the spread of a degraded form of paganism with its accompanying perversions and inversions, he would be a brave optimist who would predict a happy and peaceful future for civilization.

In spite of the sporadic efforts of internationalism, socialism, collective totemism and international crooks and cranks of every description, the world is not more united to-day than at any other period. Indeed, there was never a time when racial and class hatreds were more accentuated. Familiarity breeds contempt and also arouses jealousies. The more people rub elbows, the more they become conscious of temperamental, material and spiritual differences.

We hear a great deal about economic conditions and tariff walls as causes of wars. There is no doubt that they contribute to strife, but the fatal obstacles to peace rests with the bedeviled ideas, prejudices and passions of the human race. Such subversive qualities are nurtured on what is called history, and there is nothing more delusive or more woefully misleading than to suggest that history as it is generally known, or rather universally written, is authentic. In the distorted and prejudiced form in which it is presented, it gives rise to an exacerbated form of nationalism, essentially primitive and barbaric, that adds one more element of confusion to a hopelessly confused world.

Look at the state of Europe to-day from Sweden to the Bosporus and from Russia to Cork. Many towns and cities have been renamed in response to this nationalism, and although in some instances there may be valid reasons for the change, in others they do not exist. Exaggerated nationalism is and always has been the curse of the world. It is a fetish and like all fetishes for which men are ready to die and infinitely more ready to make other people who do not share their views die also, it is seldom founded on sound facts. There are, of course, many historic examples where tyranny and injustice have been the justifiable cause of the better forms of nationalism. But we see to-day narrow forms of this superstition, directed without any apparent sequence or issue, like the noisy dissonance of modern mechanical music.

Under such conditions, when we see so many peoples nurtured on distorted facts and erroneous ideas concerning one another, it is scarcely to be wondered at that closer acquaintance only breeds fresh bitterness and jealousy. As long as this continues, there seems little hope for the future. The next war which at the moment seems inevitable, will certainly prove fatal to our particular form of civilization, unless it collapses of its own accord from other causes.

I have already suggested what a disastrous role syphilis

plays individually and racially and indeed nationally. Alcohol is also a frequent cause of mental disturbance, hallucinations being prominent in many such cases. Intellectual disorders have provoked veritable revolutionary movements in the past; at no period have they been more in evidence than to-day. It would be a very interesting experiment to have blood tests made of some of the more prominent monsters in human shape who have convulsed society and wrought such havoc of recent years.

Many insignificant organic disorders have not infrequently led to serious consequences in past history, especially if the individual concerned exercises a preponderant influence on his social surroundings. Let me recall the remarks of Pascal concerning the stone that killed Cromwell. "Cromwell had ravaged Christianity. The Royal Family was lost, and he himself would be all powerful, but for some grains of gravel in his urethra."

It can be confidently asserted that the history of races has been notably influenced by the state of health of individuals, particularly among those who occupy responsible positions in the direction of national affairs. If these facts are admitted, and history is full of examples to prove them, the remedy suggests itself. Responsible physicians should be appointed to take an active interest in the direction of the country's business. They should have cabinet rank, and no one should be allowed to hold a responsible position whose health, as well as that of the family from which he has sprung, is not satisfactory and free from any suspicion of certain constitutional maladies.

I have said enough to show that violence, individual and collective, has frequently a pathological basis. It is therefore only common sense that medicine should be considered an auxiliary science in the management and elucidation of the highest affairs of state. If the medical profession had been consulted, it is inconceivable that Geneva with its abominable climate would have been chosen as a seat for peaceful reunions and the settlement of grave international disputes. If the great value of medical therapeutics and above all social hygiene as a preventive of wars between nations were more fully realized, there might yet be hope for the future of civilization.